AMERICAN COLLEGE LIFE

AS EDUCATION IN

WORLD OUTLOOK

Studies in
Universities and World Affairs —

AMERICAN
COLLEGE LIFE
AS EDUCATION IN
WORLD OUTLOOK

HOWARD E. WILSON

Secretary, Educational Policies Commission

AMERICAN COUNCIL ON EDUCATION · *Washington, D.C.*

Prepared for the Carnegie Endowment for International Peace; published by the American Council on Education

LIBRARY OF CONGRESS CATALOG CARD No. 56–8015

PRINTED IN THE UNITED STATES OF AMERICA

Foreword

THE CARNEGIE ENDOWMENT for International Peace has sponsored this comprehensive and provocative analysis of the part played by "outside activities" in the education of American college students. The volume is an outcome of the program on the role of colleges and universities in world affairs which was initiated five years ago by the Endowment under the direction of Dr. Wilson.

To this program, and in particular to this volume, the author has brought unusual qualifications. His experience includes association with the American Council on Education for fifteen years; for a longer period with the National Education Association, of whose Educational Policies Commission he is now executive secretary; and with the National Council for the Social Studies, of which he was a pioneering president some twenty years ago; and with other academic and international organizations. Coming to the Endowment from the faculty of the Harvard School of Education, he has been engaged in educational activities on both sides of the Atlantic; he was a member of the Endowment staff from 1945 to 1953 and since then has been a consultant. In recent years he has traveled indefatigably from campus to campus in the United States and Canada and has been a welcome and understanding guest in faculty club and student lounge.

The contributions of the "cocurricular" and the "extracurricular" on the modern campus are often taken for granted or dismissed as irrelevant if not detrimental to education. Dr. Wilson's volume subjects the actual contribution—and especially the potential role—to searching appraisal. Written with an eye to education in world affairs, it will clearly be of value to specialists in that field. There are, moreover, broad implications in the volume which should be of interest to all college teachers and administrators who are concerned with the full educational effectiveness of the institutions they serve.

JOSEPH E. JOHNSON, *President*
Carnegie Endowment for International Peace

Preface

COLLEGES AND universities have a major role to play in the complex process by which modern nations conduct their relations with each other. Institutions of higher education both reflect and help to shape the cultures and the policies of their supporting societies. They are nerve centers in the continual adaptation of nations to the emerging realities of international life. In one sense they are buffers between a complex present and an uncertain future.

American institutions of higher education educate the men and women who are to become most influential in determining public opinion and national policy respecting international matters. They educate the specialists in international relations and promote the development of studies on which the new field of specialization is based. Most of the research on international politics, law, organization, and on the psychology of peoples, and much of the scientific research increasingly essential to the national security is conducted within universities. Academic personnel is continually called into the public service both in formulating and in implementing policy. Colleges and universities are deeply involved in programs for interchange of persons. Voices from the campus have a significant part in adult education about world affairs, and universities maintain programs reaching large off-campus audiences. In such conflicts of ideas and ideals as today lie close to the surface of international affairs, the very substance of the colleges and universities—the arts and the sciences and the professions—are themselves involved in the conduct of national and international policies.

Nations demand much from modern universities, and the institutions themselves have a heavy stake in the conduct of foreign affairs. The demands of manpower for national security fall particularly heavily on the college and university population. Most of the education for civilized living to which universities and colleges are devoted is predicated upon avoidance of war. The economic bases of American higher education, as, indeed, of the nation as a whole, will not easily weather further costly international conflict. The intellectual freedom on which university life rests is at issue in the conflicts of our times. In self-interest, even if for no other reason, universities and colleges are deeply concerned with the conduct of world affairs.

With such general considerations as these the Carnegie Endowment for International Peace has long been involved. Through four critical decades since 1911 it has aided in developing systematic study of international relations and has been concerned with the increasing impact of international events on American life, including American academic life. In 1950, partly in logical development from its own experience and partly out of the expressed concern of many academic leaders over the varieties and vagaries of educational adjustments to America's new role in international relations, the Endowment undertook a program of study of American universities and world affairs.

The first phase of the program was conducted by the Endowment in cooperation with eight selected institutions of higher education, each of which made an exploratory inventory and analysis of its resources and activities bearing on world affairs. Faculty committees in each institution, representative of the whole institution, were set up; in cooperation with Endowment consultants, these committees explored the developments in their institutions bearing on world affairs. They raised questions which need to be answered by academic communities. Their work is briefly reported in *Universities and World*

Affairs,[1] published by the Endowment in 1951. The volume indicated that the self-survey approach was fruitful, and it provided a kind of handbook for self-survey groups in other institutions.

Following publication of the introductory handbook, a series of thirteen regional conferences was sponsored by the Endowment at which representatives of faculty and administration from three hundred colleges and universities discussed the possibilities of self-surveys and appraisals. A group of almost one hundred institutions, widely distributed as to location, size, and character, decided to make such self-analyses; the Endowment cooperated with them between 1952 and 1955 by providing a clearinghouse service and a limited measure of consultation. Sixty institutions have since then completed their self-surveys, and their reports have been distributed as mimeographed documents to cooperating institutions.

The institutional reports vary widely in scope, method, and merit, for a basic characteristic of the total program has been its decentralized character. The Endowment did not propose to the institutions a recommended academic plan of action; it sought only to have each institution raise the right questions in this field, and then to formulate the answers which seemed to have greatest validity within the particular institutional context. The self-survey activities were neither standardized in form nor intended to produce a platform of recommendations for other institutions to follow. It was hoped that they would set in motion constructive developments in the processes by which each campus adjusts in its own way to the impact of world affairs. There is evidence that, in many cases, the hope is in process of achievement.

Another basic characteristic of the survey program was an institutional, as contrasted with a disciplinary, focus. The project

[1] Howard E. Wilson, *Universities and World Affairs* (New York: Carnegie Endowment for International Peace, 1951), 88 pp.

was only in part an analysis of what is being taught in courses in international relations or of the status of such courses in the curriculum. The project sought to view the college or university as a whole, as it is seen by administrative leaders and trustees. The surveys dealt with instructional activities, research enterprises, interchange of persons, informal extracurricular and cocurricular affairs in college life, and the role of the institution in adult thinking. They dealt with all the ways and phases of academic existence by which the university is affected or by which it affects the formulation of foreign policy and the conduct of world affairs. Such a cross-sectional, institution-wide approach is a sociological analysis of how an institution is related to the great international currents of contemporary life.

Such a survey-appraisal is certainly not easy to develop and cannot be fully precise in its outcome. Even so, such an approach seems today to be advantageous and almost necessary. Colleges and universities have perhaps undertaken some responsibilities unwisely, may have neglected others, have frequently failed to coordinate their own enterprises, have sometimes overextended themselves or have failed to utilize adequately some resources which have developed under the international interests and pressures of recent years. To take stock of what has been done and to focus attention on what is most important, to coordinate efforts which are mutually supportive, to use the available academic resources most adequately and wisely are but common sense in view of the international problems, both for society and for institutions of higher education, that lie ahead.

An interpretation of the survey experience on widely varied campuses has implication and suggestion for American higher education in general. To secure this intepretation, not merely as a report on a project, but as seen in relation to other studies and developments, the Endowment requested a number of specialists to prepare volumes on topics which had been revealed in the surveys as particularly impórtant. The resulting series of books, of which this is one, is published by the American Council on Education as a contribution to thought about higher education in America today. Each of these volumes draws fully on the self-surveys and appraisals made by institutions which have cooperated in the Endowment's program but is in no sense limited to these surveys. The author or authors of each volume have been free to develop the most constructive treatment possible of the topics with which they deal. A list of the authors and titles of the books in the series is found on page ii of this volume.

The present volume, *American College Life as Education in World Outlook*, deals with many of the informal forces and influences which condition the education of college men and women. There is no implication in the volume that extracurricular activities are more influential than is the curriculum; indeed, the basic thesis to which the first chapter is devoted is that curriculum and extracurriculum are, or ought to be, closely interrelated. Chapter 1 presents a concept of collegiate life and an analysis of its historical development and trends in the United States; chapter 2 discusses certain physical facilities for informal learning which characterize most campuses; chapter 3 deals with the members of the college as resources for informal education about world affairs; chapter 4 describes student activities which influence world outlook; chapter 5 deals with student travel as an academic phenomenon; and chapter 6 discusses means by which college life may be better organized in focus on more worthy ends. Chapter 1 deals primarily with a broadly educational concept, and the succeeding chapters emphasize the relation of this concept to the specific task of education about world affairs. Education about world affairs is dealt with in its setting as one facet or focus of the total experience of going to college.

The terms "world affairs" and "international relations" are used in this volume in their broadest sense. They include not only the politics of intergovernmental relations and the economics of international life, but also the cultural contacts and interpenetrations of peoples in contact with peoples. Education for world affairs includes the understanding and attitudes students acquire respecting other cultures or world areas, and it includes understanding and feeling about America's position in the international situation. This volume deals with education about world affairs as part of a more general concept of life in the modern world. It seeks to deal with the informal collegiate influences which condition students' outlook, both emotional and intellectual, toward all the ramifications of relations among twentieth-century nations and cultures.

HOWARD E. WILSON

Washington, D.C.
September 15, 1955

Acknowledgments

MY SENSE of indebtedness for the materials presented in this volume extends to many friends—to my colleagues at the Carnegie Endowment, particularly James T. Shotwell, Joseph E. Johnson, William G. Avirett, Anne Winslow, and Lawrence Finkelstein; to the committees and individual faculty members in the colleges and universities which cooperated with the Endowment in evaluating their resources and activities bearing on world affairs; to the authors of other volumes in this series; to students on many campuses who have shared their outlooks with me; and especially to Florence Heden Wilson, Henry W. Holmes, Gordon Samson, and Lillian S. Parker, whose continued counsel and assistance have been invaluable.

I gratefully acknowledge the contributions of all these and other friends, while reserving to myself full responsibility for the shortcomings in this volume.

H. E. W.

Contents

List of Tables

Campus and Classroom

The American college—"the despair of educational reformers and logical pedagogues, the astonishment of continental scholars; a place which is neither a house of learning nor a house of play, but a little of both; and withal a microcosm of the world in which we live."—Samuel Eliot Morison, Founding of Harvard

To LOOK at films on college life produced by the sages of Hollywood and then to read the college catalogues which describe academic courses and curricular patterns is to begin to understand the significant meaning of the title of Burges Johnson's book, *Campus versus Classroom.*[1] There is an unfortunate dichotomy in the life of college students—a bifurcation in the college itself which has serious repercussions in every phase of higher education.

For Hollywood, for the popular magazines, for some students, and for a larger number of alumni, college is in essence a series of romantic escapades, punctuated with athletic crises. For many students, either in the small college or in the undergraduate division of a great university, the student activities of college life are so challenging and powerful as to be the dominant influence in "higher" education. To many Americans these

[1] Johnson, *Campus versus Classroom* (New York: Ives Washburn, Inc., 1946).

1

collegiate activities are adequately justified as the real "preparation for life" in a competitive society. Students with this concept of college set themselves goals of getting on the team, of winning a student election, or of gaining a post on the staff of the student newspaper. These are the students who, as Canby points out in his reminiscences of Yale, sing "not for sweet music's sake, but to 'make' the glee club." [2] For other students of course, life is a "grind," a serious business of study, sometimes for sober intellect's sake but more often for utilitarian purposes connected with vocational ambition. Woodrow Wilson wrote in 1909, "The work of the college, the work of its classrooms and laboratories, has become the merely formal and compulsory side of its life . . . a score of other things, lumped under the term 'undergraduate activities' have become the vital spontaneous, absorbing realities for nine out of ten men who go to college." [3] Whether college work or college life is more powerful in that education of students which involves the inculcation of enduring values and standards and insights it would be difficult to say.

This "problem of the unintegrated college" is one of the major troubles in higher education in the United States today. American colleges and universities—large or small, rural or urban, public or private, vocational or nonvocational—have drifted into a situation in which the curriculum and the extracurriculum are too frequently working at cross-purposes. The problem posed by this dichotomy is not solved or eliminated either by denouncing with scholarly dudgeon the false gods of the extracurriculum or relaxing in alumnal nostalgia over student activities as an exciting and irresponsible prelude to the serious perplexities of adult life.

The fact is that in America we are committed to the concept

[2] Henry Seidel Canby, Alma Mater: The Gothic Age of the American College (New York: Farrar & Rinehart, 1936), p. 37.

[3] Wilson, "What Is College For?" Scribner's Magazine, November 1909, p. 576.

of an all-embracing "college life" as good education, but in the actuality of college living its divers chords and melodies are too rarely orchestrated. The resultant disharmony reverberates in both the procedures and the products of higher education. Many of the problems of academic life—as for example, the search for the meaning of a "liberal" education—cannot be solved until we have found some basis on which college life itself may be more adequately integrated. One cannot deal realistically with the problems of education about world affairs for the college men and women of America, or of education for economic literacy, or of education in literary taste, or of training in reflective thought without recognizing, and in some degree harmonizing, the varied, now too frequently conflicting, elements in the totality of our academic life.

In order to deal adequately with the possibilities of college-level education in any of its functions, it is necessary to deal both with the curriculum and the extracurriculum, and with the relationship between the two. It is essential to recognize the total experience of the "college way of life" as an educative experience, powerful in its shaping of mind and emotions.

Mather's "Collegiate Way of Living"

The history of American academic institutions, even briefly examined, is illuminating on this matter. Early American colleges derived their character very largely from the tradition of the English public schools and the residential colleges of Cambridge and Oxford. They were, of course, shaped and colored by the dominating religious interests of the colonial era. Harvard, William and Mary, Yale, Columbia, Princeton, and Brown were all set up not only as centers of instruction but also consciously as planned ways of living for students. Students were then markedly younger than present-day students and were less widely representative of all levels of the population; they were, by home and society, committed to a religious orthodoxy to which the institutions were also committed. The masters of these early colleges promulgated detailed regulations for what Cotton Mather in the *Magnalia* called the "collegiate way of living,"[4] prescribing manners and morals and activities and studies, all of a relatively consistent, integrated pattern. Life in President Dunster's "yard" at Harvard or in the manse which previsaged Princeton was unified even though rigid and orthodox and, by our standards, unpleasant. The founders of American colleges recognized no divergence between curriculum and extracurriculum, as the "inmates of the college" were sternly aware.

The point of view of the early college authorities, which was characteristic of most institutions through the first half of the nineteenth century, was expressed by President Dunster at Harvard in 1642. He announced the requirements for graduation from Harvard by writing that:

> Every scholar that by proof is found able to translate the original of the Old and New Testament into the Latin tongue, and to resolve them logically, and shall be imbued with the beginnings of natural and moral philosophy, *withall being of honest life and conversation,* and at any public act hath the appreciation of the Overseers and

---

[4] "It was not only natural that Harvard should copy an English college in aims, curriculum, and manner of life and discipline. It was a matter of deliberate design. It might have been much easier for the poorly-endowed school to board out its students with the townspeople, according to the custom of universities in the Netherlands, with which the founders were familiar. This was actually suggested by one Emmanuel Downing, who thought it was enough to hire some ministers to read a weekly lesson on 'logick, greke or hebrew' and let the students shift for themselves. But, as Cotton Mather observed, 'the Government of New England was for having their students brought up in a more Collegiate Way of Living.' It was regarded as an educational imperative. So, in the sense that the curriculum refers to all of the educational influences surrounding the student, housing and out-of-class activities were not then regarded as 'extra-curricular.'" Clyde Sanfred Johnson, "Student Self-government: A Preliminary Survey of the Background and Development of Extra-class Activities at the University of California, Los Angeles" (Doctoral thesis, University of California, Los Angeles, 1948), p. 12.

Masters of the College, may be invested with his first degree; but no one will expect this degree until he shall have passed four years in college *and has maintained therein a blameless life and has sedulously observed all public exercises.*[5]

And it is said of Dunster that "no possible conduct escaped his eye. Class deportment, plan of studies, personal habits, daily life, private devotions, social intercourse, and civil privileges, were all directed." [6] Student reactions to these controls were varied. That form of integrated experience which can take place only within the individual learner may have been quite rare. But the controllers and planners of early American college education saw both curriculum and extracurriculum as fundamental parts of one whole for which they accepted responsibility.

In the early decades of the nineteenth century, with colleges largely founded and dominated by religious sects, this repressive but unified collegiate concept followed the path of manifest destiny westward. The early history of Illinois College, founded in Jacksonville by a "Yale band" of young missionaries trained in the orthodoxy of New Haven, with one of the Beechers as its first president, illustrates this development. Every detail of the curriculum in the frontier college was prescribed along the lines of the 1828 report of the Yale faculty in support of the traditional classical studies, and also "professors inquired minutely into the daily life of students; rules and restrictions were numerous. . . . The religious life of the students was carefully and even strenuously regulated." [7]

The schedule of college life extended from waking hours to the evening curfew; there was a determined effort to regiment the whole of student existence. Such matters of personal be-

[5] Quoted by Agatho Zimmer in *Changing Concepts of Higher Education in America Since 1700* (Washington: Catholic University of America, 1938), pp. 50–51.

[6] Quoted by John Marshall Barker in *Colleges in America* (Cleveland, Ohio: Cleveland Printing & Publishing Co., 1893), p. 89.

[7] Charles Henry Rammelkamp, *Illinois College: A Centennial History, 1829–1929* (New Haven, Conn.: Yale University Press, 1928), p. 77.

havior as praying or swearing, selling one's possessions, or leaving the campus for a visit in town were regulated. Published rules and regulations for behavior in college grew increasingly elaborate and detailed. Early in the nineteenth century the Laws of Union College contained eleven chapters of from seven to twenty-three sections each. Page after page of official rules were common in college; they dealt with every phase of behavior in the college community; and students were expected to know them and to observe them under penalty of discipline.[8]

As Burges Johnson has pointed out, in the volume already referred to, *Campus versus Classroom:*

The young men who first graduated from our colleges were trained by both classroom and campus while the two had unity. The campus successfully kept them loyal to the church. Its prayer meetings, revival services, debating societies, discussion groups, and compulsory daily chapel dovetailed with a classroom which sought first of all to sustain the old theology and harmonize all knowledge with existing religious belief.[9]

[8] "The system of rules governing the student were as doctrinaire and unrealistic as the curriculum and the system of multitudinous religious services. His whole life was regimented from the time he arose at 4:30 or 5:00 until the compulsory bedtime at 9:00 or 10:00. The usual schedule provided for morning and evening prayers; two or three recitation periods, one or two in the morning, the other in the afternoon; a morning and afternoon study period (not always used for that purpose), at least one being two hours long; breakfast, dinner and supper. This left three free periods, one in the morning, one from noon to two, and the third from evening prayers to 7:00 in winter, 9:00 in the summer. As late as 1841 almost the same schedule was decreed by the Regents of the new University of Michigan. In Northern colleges the student often used his free morning period to cut firewood and lug it up to his room. Even his leisure time was hedged about with multiple restrictions. The earliest Harvard students were commanded to pray in secret and read scriptures twice a day. Not only was swearing forbidden, but also all idle, foolish, bitter, scoffing, frothy and wanton words—rather a blanket coverage of normal student conversation. Students were forbidden to sell or exchange articles above the value of 6d, and could not go to town without permission from a college official." Ernest P. Earnest, *Academic Procession: An Informal History of the American College, 1636 to 1953* (Indianapolis, Ind.: Bobbs-Merrill Co., 1953), pp. 41–42.

[9] Burges Johnson, *op. cit.,* p. 53.

Reactions against the rigid controls of early college life were, of course, pronounced and numerous. Student riots over curfew regulations, over required attendance at prayers, over the food in commons, and over all the restrictions on behavior which were covered in the lengthy compendiums of regulations were common. In the light of these reactions, the life of a conscientious professor, like that of Gilbert and Sullivan's policeman, "was not a happy one." So determined were student objections to the rigid controls of college life that the faculty member seemed often fully as much a policeman as a professor.

"Campus versus Classroom"

The rift between students and professors widened as the nineteenth century brought sweeping changes in American society and in academic concepts. A decline in religious orthodoxy in society at large took from college life the chief prop of its authoritarianism. The rapid settling of the continent; the great humanitarian and social reform movements of the 1840's and 1850's; the changing status of women in society; the surging changes brought on by the War between the States; and particularly the rise of gigantic industrial and commercial forces— all altered American society, and with it American academic life. Fewer college students were concerned with a ministerial career and more were caught up in the industrial vitality of a growing country. Colleges, and particularly the great state universities which rose in the Middle West of the mid-nineteenth century, drew their clientele from wider segments of the population; students entered college with more varied backgrounds and experiences and interests and purposes. Women were admitted either to separate colleges or to the growing number of coeducational institutions.

As the separation between the traditional curriculum and the dominant interests of American society became more pronounced, college enrollments declined for a time. Fundamental adjustments had to be made in academic concepts before colleges and universities again expanded and won the prestige they now enjoy. The presidents of Columbia and Brown and Michigan and Cornell pioneered in rethinking during the middle decades of the nineteenth century the nature and function of their institutions. Within the curriculum a sweeping conflict over a prescribed, as against an elective, system of studies emerged in Ticknor's Harvard as early as 1825 and in the foundation years of Jefferson's University of Virginia. By the end of the century the elective system became a dominant reform under the leadership of Charles W. Eliot.[10] The relative freedom of the student in choice of courses which was brought in from German universities was an influence against the tradition of the English residential college. As *Lernfreiheit*, the right to study subjects of one's own choice, the elective system seemed a form of academic freedom.

Throughout the nineteenth century, the college and university were in ferment and transition. With the gradual abandonment of the traditional classical and theological curriculums, with the systematic attempt to relate educational institutions more intimately to the civic and industrial movements of a rapidly growing society, and with the rise of German influence on American education, the orthodox unity which had been sought as well as the rigidity which had been imposed in the life of early colleges disappeared. For a time the ascendancy of residential colleges was halted; the University of Michigan was planned, for example, as an institution without dormitories and dining halls. An outstanding president in Ann Arbor

set about building Michigan on the German pattern. Arguing that it was not the function of a university to provide board and lodging, he

[10] See R. Freeman Butts, *The College Charts Its Course: Historical Conceptions and Current Proposals* (New York: McGraw-Hill Book Co., 1939).

abolished dormitories and used the space for a library, museum of natural history, and art gallery. The change was vastly more radical than a mere shift of students to town boarding houses; it ran counter to the whole *in loco parentis* philosophy of American colleges.[11]

A revolution in higher education in America was under way. During the second half of the nineteenth century new institutions were founded, each with its own emphasis and philosophy— Cornell, Johns Hopkins, Stanford, Chicago, Vassar, Wellesley, Smith, Barnard, Radcliffe, many of the great state universities, and all of the land-grant colleges. A vast public school system recruited more widely for the colleges and gave to the institutions older students better prepared in many ways for college work. Eliot at Harvard, Gilman at Hopkins, White at Cornell, Tappan and Angell at Michigan, Van Hise at Wisconsin, Harper at Chicago were creatively remolding American academic institutions, with a needed emphasis on a curriculum which recognized the natural and social sciences, and which brought higher education into the service of a society whose temper was pragmatic and utilitarian. Not unconcerned with the college way of life, their chief emphasis, however, was entirely on curriculum reform, research enterprises, and the development of universities, comprehensive and attuned to emerging American life.

Widely, and with great relief for the most part, faculties relinquished most of their meticulous, exhausting, and thankless police functions. Compulsory prayers and chapel were generally abandoned. The compendiums of detailed regulations became shorter and simpler or disappeared entirely. With the rise of universities in the modern sense, heavily influenced by the research interests of graduate schools, the faculties of American institutions of higher education became increasingly absorbed in the scholarship of their divers academic inquiries. The curriculum became for them, in a sense, the whole institution. With

[11] Earnest, *op. cit.*, pp. 71–72.

the decline of classical studies in the curriculum, and the extraordinary developments in the sciences, both natural and social, the opportunities and demands of scholarship multiplied. Specialization increased, and the faculty member became increasingly absorbed in his own section of the library and laboratory. With the rise of research interests, the lecture system in teaching, and the wide-ranging challenges of the elective system by which "equivalence of subjects" was recognized, ambitious faculty members seemed increasingly removed from the contacts and context of teaching. The gap between students and faculty, between curriculum and extracurriculum grew wider. By the first decade of the twentieth century, Woodrow Wilson could refer to "study" as an interruption to "college life." The faculty, with little part in that life, "organized the interruption." What was an "interruption" for many students was itself increasingly the college life to which the faculty gave allegiance. As a later analyst observed, "Preoccupied solely with intellectual matters, the faculty attitude was that of laissez-faire with respect to the clubs and associations of undergraduates." [12]

Student Life

Even while an academic revolution was remaking the curriculum in a reflection of American society and in terms more congenial to many students, most students found new, non-curricular activities of an absorbing nature. The decline of faculty interest in and concern with activities beyond the formal curriculum did not mean any decline in the number and influence of such activities. On the contrary, the "activities" of college life proliferated and grew increasingly absorbing as faculty controls were relaxed. During the period from about 1880 to about 1930, college life—by then synonymous with *student* life—took on a

[12] Clyde Sanfred Johnson, *op. cit.*, p. 55.

vitality and glamour seldom equaled. As Ernest Earnest has pointed out:

> Probably in no period in the history of the American college has men's student life been so carefree, so much a world in itself. The old puritanism had relaxed; the passions of the Civil War had subsided; the later concern over social and economic problems had—at least at men's colleges—not yet impinged. "We toil not, neither do we agitate, but we play football" was the boast of the Yale class of 1901. All over the nation students could have made the same statement.[13]

Life at Yale at the turn of the century has been memorably described by Henry Seidel Canby in *Alma Mater: The Gothic Age of the American College*, an illuminating volume both for the social historian and for the educational philosopher. He describes the experience of attending college as being

> so highly charged with emotion, so powerful in its influences on behavior, that it may be said to have been one hundred percent efficient at a time when higher education in the sense common to all the ages had touched only here and there American habits of thought

at the undergraduate level. With nostalgia and affection and objective criticism, Canby referred to the American college of 1900

> which was not a collegium of letters but rather a society for competitive education; not an association of scholars but rather a coming together of youths preparing to be capitalists; and yet not a utilitarian institution so much as a Utopia for those who later would play all life like a strenuous game; this college, which was not sordid, not isolated entirely from movements of beauty and the mind, was so impure a mixture that its influences were sure to break up into compounds of unusual intricacy, poisons and explosives among them.[14]

During the era of which Canby wrote, he suggests that typical students devoted about 90 percent of their time and energies to the activities which prepared them for what Theodore Roose-

[13] Earnest, *op. cit.*, pp. 230–31.
[14] Canby, *op. cit.*, pp. 98–99.

velt, in the same era, called "the strenuous life." By intense
activity in clubs and athletics, fraternities and literary societies,
and social and campus events, the student demonstrated his
ability to his peers in terms convincing to them, evidenced his
wholehearted and evangelistic loyalty to his chosen alma mater,
won the success which had prestige and promise for the future,
and prepared himself for a career in strenuous, dynamic America. In a sense, students sought in strenuous college activity a
reality missing in much of the curriculum to which they were
exposed. Their activities were not all anti-intellectual; the
widespread literary societies provided, in some ways, an intellectual fare more vital than the classroom offered.

The activities which seemed to the student—and in many
cases to his parents—to be at the heart of his "real" education
were not those of the academic classroom or those in which the
faculty members ordinarily had much part. His "higher education" was in the turmoil of "student life"; it seemed to emphasize a separation of the young from the experience and the
interests of the older; his college was not a "community of
scholars, young and old," but a community of the young, some
of whom, at least, had rudimentary scholarly interests. To quote
again from Canby, describing a Yale which did not differ
basically from other colleges and universities throughout the
nation in 1900:

> The cry in our undergraduate world was always "do something,"
> "what does he do?" Freshmen hurried up and down entry stairs
> seeking news for the college paper, athletes . . . struggled . . . to get
> or hold places on the teams, boys with rudiments of business ability
> were managers of magazines, orchestras, teams, or cooperative pants-
> pressing companies. . . . Long throats went in for social drinking,
> glib minds for politics; everything but scholarship was in my day an
> "activity" and called "doing something for the college." . . . The
> environment was too powerful. . . . College life was so vital in itself
> and so formative that ideas, the search for truth, scholarship, and the
> forecasts and interpretations of the intellect in general, were inevitably
> mere by-products of an institution whose service was to teach com-

petition and the public school code. . . . College life was the heart of the educational machine.[15]

Student life, as portrayed in the literature on Stover at Yale or Rogers at Harvard or as described by Fitzgerald at Princeton and as developed throughout America in the second and third decades of the present century, became very generally a thing apart from the stated and long-term interests and functions of higher education. It was the period of the "gentleman's C" and of the rise of tutoring schools near many campuses, where gentlemen paid "grinds" to conduct pre-examination cramming sessions. Literary societies began to die out, and athletic and social events moved to a new pre-eminence. Changes in American society, coming to a head in the 1920's and violently reflected in the mores of student behavior, brought excesses. The "noble experiment" of prohibition, the gross commercialization of sports, the popularization of the motor car, changes in family life, the inevitable aftermath of World War I, all led to the collegiate era of coonskin coats, hip flasks, flappers, necking, and the greatest football spectacles of all time. Yet the importance of these excesses can be easily exaggerated; they were probably no more excessive than the earlier revolts against Puritan controls. The important matter is that for very many students in America for whom college life was an energetic escapade, this life had very little relation to the academic interests of the college faculty.

It is easy, of course, to exaggerate this separation. In the case of many individual students, fortunate in their instructors and in their extracurricular interests, college was an outstanding intellectual and aesthetic experience. As Hofstadter and Hardy point out:

Brilliant and cultivated men, even brilliant rebels against the colleges themselves, came out of the old schools. Informal association then as always meant a great deal in the educative process. The

[15] *Ibid.*, pp. 37–38, 78–79.

collegiate way of life, with its sense of community, was an educational as well as a social force. Students found in their debating societies a particularly satisfying way of sharpening their minds, intensifying their capacity for analysis, and exercising their spontaneous interests. Good teachers did emerge. Occasionally, where courses in moral philosophy were taught by men of the capacity of Wayland and March, they opened large intellectual vistas.[16]

Yet with all the individual exceptions, and recognizing that, as Canby said of Yale, college life was "not isolated entirely from movements of beauty and the mind," the general separation between faculty interests and student life was a striking characteristic of late nineteenth-century higher education in America.

Analyzing Campus Mores

The gap between curriculum and extracurriculum which had widened steadily during the nineteenth century came under increasing scrutiny as both the curriculum and the extracurriculum began to show signs of strain and excess during the first half of the twentieth century. On the academic side, the elective system led to what various observers have called the cafeteria program in higher education. The proliferation of courses, based both on increased specialization in scholarship and on the attempt to make higher education contribute to every exigency of man in modern society, created a well-nigh unmanageable academic structure. As Charles and Mary Beard pointed out in *The Rise of American Civilization:*

> Learning itself, always subdued more or less to the major concerns of its age, bent like a reed before new demands as the curricula of colleges underwent changes adapted to an age of industry. . . . Courses of instruction were divided and subdivided, dissolving earlier philosophies of life and practice, and multiplying academic goods almost as rapidly as inventors multiplied material commodities.[17]

[16] Richard Hofstadter and C. DeWitt Hardy, *The Development and Scope of Higher Education in the United States* (New York: Columbia University Press, 1952), pp. 20–21.

[17] Charles A. Beard and Mary R. Beard, *The Rise of American Civilization* (New York: Macmillan Co., 1927), II, 794–95.

On the side of "student life," the scandals of commercialized athletics and the breakdown of old social controls created a campus culture hardly justifiable under educational standards. Beginning seriously with the onset of the depression in the 1930's and accelerated by the problems and crises of peace and war which have tended to mature American society since that time, the forces of higher education have moved, often unconsciously, toward a better integration of the collegiate way of life—not a revival of a colonial pattern but an adaptation of college life to the realities of contemporary America.

For one thing, serious scholars began to study the student life which had emerged in our institutions. Canby wrote his delightful reminiscent volume in 1936; it was a literary and individual expression of sociological points of view formulated a decade earlier by Robert Cooley Angell in *The Campus: A Study of Contemporary Undergraduate Life in the American University*. Angell, on the basis of polls and surveys, described what students were reading—and were not reading; he analyzed student clubs and indicated student values and outlooks. He suggested in terms reminiscent of the medieval university that:

There is a not uncommon feeling that a state of war exists between faculty members and students—no mere game, where the canons of sportsmanship prevail, but a downright ruthless struggle in which any method of overcoming the foe is justified. . . . The absence of scholarly morale indicates a fundamental maladjustment between the institution of higher education and its members. A great many undergraduates have not the true purposes of a university at heart; they are in the institution but not of it. . . . Hence we have a great body of students united insofar as they are united at all, not by the central purpose of the university but rather by by-products like athletics.[18]

During the period of the 1920's, Francis S. Chapin and O. M. Mehus conducted systematic studies of student life at the

[18] Angell, *The Campus: A Study of Contemporary Undergraduate Life in the American University* (New York: D. Appleton-Century, 1928), pp. 44, 212.

University of Minnesota; [19] Edward Hartshorne wrote on "Undergraduate Society and the College Culture"; [20] Katzfi Allport, and Jenness made comprehensive studies of student attitudes at Syracuse University; [21] Heber Harper studied the attitudes of college students toward foreign policy and international relations and probed to discern the sources of these attitudes in the experiences of college life. [22] James Wechsler described *Revolt on the Campus;* [23] Percy Marks vigorously raised the question *Which Way Parnassus?* [24] Reminiscent and autobiographical volumes by Bliss Perry, Irwin Edman, and Christian Gauss, among others, cast light on the nature of the academic societies we had produced. James Hawes wrote in 1929 of *Twenty Years Among the Twenty Year Olds,* [25] half-unconsciously expressing the values and mores of the fraternity system. By the 1940's Logan Wilson was writing a sociological analysis of *The Academic Man;* [26] Ruth Strang was discussing *Group Activities in College and Secondary School;* [27] and Janet Kelley analyzed *College Life and the Mores.* [28] As Cowley pointed out in 1945,

[19] Chapin and Mehus, *Extra-Curricular Activities at the University of Minnesota* (Minneapolis: University of Minnesota Press, 1929).

[20] Hartshorne, "Undergraduate Society and the College Culture," *American Sociological Review,* June 1943, pp. 321–32.

[21] Daniel Katz, F. H. Allport, and M. B. Jenness, *Students' Attitudes: A Report of the Syracuse University Reaction Study* (Syracuse, N.Y.: W. E. Mosher, Syracuse University, 1931).

[22] Harper, *What European and American Students Think on International Problems: A Comparative Study of the World-Mindedness of University Students,* Studies of the International Institute, No. 12 (New York: Teachers College, Columbia University, 1931).

[23] Wechsler, *Revolt on the Campus* (New York: Covici Friede, Inc., 1935).

[24] Marks, *Which Way Parnassus?* (New York: Harcourt Brace & Co., 1926).

[25] Hawes, *Twenty Years Among the Twenty Year Olds: A Story of Our Colleges of Today* (New York: E. P. Dutton Co., 1929).

[26] Wilson, *The Academic Man: A Study in the Sociology of a Profession* (New York: Oxford University Press, 1942).

[27] Strang, *Group Activities in College and Secondary School* (Rev. ed.; New York: Harper & Bros., 1946).

[28] Kelley, *College Life and the Mores* (New York: Bureau of Publications, Teachers College, Columbia University, 1949).

study of college mores could not be limited to "such superficial expressions as college songs, cheers, or rally bonfires." Rather, mores were recognized as "kinds of social energy which determined the intellectual, social, and moral tones of every college and university campus." [29]

Although interrupted by depression and by war, the movement for realistic analysis of the culture patterns of college life gathered momentum after the early 1920's. Sociology, psychology, literature, history, anthropology, all contributed to the analysis. By the 1950's an observer lived in expectation that a cultural anthropologist would before too long stay home from Samoa or Borneo or New Guinea, or even from Middletown and Yankee City, long enough to dissect the processes of "coming of age" on an American college campus.

Academic Reform Movements

Beginning also in the years following World War I, a group of educational pioneers formulated academic reforms which tended toward the focusing of all phases of college life on intellectual and aesthetic concerns. Describing the philosophy of Frank Aydelotte as he set about remolding Swarthmore, [30] his colleagues emphasized that the college "can arrange a setting" which will conduce to the fullest development of individuals intellectually as well as morally. Many of the reform and developmental programs in American higher education of the last three decades have sought to "arrange a setting" in which the prestige of intellectual activity might be increased and strengthened within the accepted values and mores of the campus. The Swarthmore honors plan had the effect not only of reforming the curriculum for selected students, but of creating a cam-

[29] William H. Cowley, "Challenge to Physical Education," *Journal of Higher Education*, April 1945, p. 175.

[30] Swarthmore College Faculty, *An Adventure in Education: Swarthmore College Under Frank Aydelotte* (New York: Macmillan Co., 1941).

pus way of life in which prestige was accorded the great traditions of learning and of universities. It had the effect of integrating curriculum and extracurriculum by reforms in both.

In various ways, but toward the same end, changes were made in established institutions, and new institutions were founded. The preceptorial plan at Princeton, the tutorial plan at Harvard, the faculty-student congress at Bucknell, the study-work plan at Antioch, all affected the mores of college life and gave increased prestige to "things of beauty and of the mind" among students and faculty alike. The house plan at Harvard and Yale, developed through gifts of Harkness, is an example of the adaptation of the residential college to modern circumstances. Its emphasis on the tutorial system brings students and faculty into closer relationship and enhances the life of serious learning as a phase of college life. The very architecture with which Stanford was endowed at birth, with its quads and cloisters, reflects the same concern. The uniquely American development of student centers in the model of those at Cornell and Wisconsin is again one approach to the focusing of student activities on goals shared by faculty as well as undergraduates, as will be demonstrated later. Meiklejohn's program at Amherst, and later at Wisconsin, intended to develop a zest for things intellectual, was, with all its vicissitudes, an experiment tending in the direction toward which American academic life was turning.

During these same years, various new institutions were created, designed to reintegrate the "society of scholars, young and old." Opening in 1928, Sarah Lawrence College drew on the theories of John Dewey in developing an educational program which harnessed student thought with campus and community experience. At Bennington, Reed, Goddard, Black Mountain, Rollins, and elsewhere, institutions came into existence in a pattern designed to reduce the internal conflicts and confusions and to increase the cultural effectiveness of college life. Not all the experiments fully attained their aims, but they came as response to a need deeply felt in American academic life and impelled by basic social trends of the nation.

Deans of Students

Another influence tending toward the integration of campus and classroom was the rise of personnel services as a distinctive feature of American higher education. Concern with the problems of an individual student who was beset by the difficulties of adjustment within a somewhat hectic and fragmented college community and who needed the mature guidance which alone could make the elective system of the curriculum advantageous led to the development of the work of "deans of students" and to extensive counseling and guidance services. Ralph McDonald describes the movement by saying:

> The expansion almost ad infinitum of courses and programs literally forced American colleges and universities during the first half of the twentieth century to discover the individual student. In 1900 individual measurement and guidance were almost unknown, but by 1950 programs of counseling were found throughout the country. The recognition of individual differences and the need for the development of the whole person have changed very substantially the procedures and practices in higher-education institutions. A great host of student-personnel workers have been added to our college staffs to help accomplish these worthwhile purposes.[31]

The personnel and guidance movement, arising both from a concern with the individual in an increasingly impersonal society and from a reaction to the complexities and excesses which had come to characterize curriculum and extracurriculum alike, was initially concerned with the student rather than with college life. But in advancing the development of the individual, the personnel worker was inevitably led into analysis of the mores of college life and ultimately into concern with

[31] McDonald, "A Half Century of American Higher Education—1900 to 1950," *Association of American Colleges Bulletin*, October 1954, p. 352.

the life of the whole institution. As this concern led from the individual—even the individual statistically considered—into his social context, it was at first primarily concerned with "student life." Only gradually did the personnel movement come to deal with the life of the total college, including the interrelations between older and younger members of the college community, and between curriculum and extracurriculum.

The development of the counseling program from a concern with the individual toward a relatively scientific concern with the totality of the collegiate way of life is well illustrated in the series of reports issued since 1939 by the Committee on Student Personnel Work of the American Council of Education. In a 1952 report on *Student Personnel Programs in Transition* it is emphasized that such programs must deal with every aspect of the college environment, "both those aspects found in the college classroom and those found outside the classroom."

The personnel point of view actually takes into consideration every department and every function of the college. Administrative offices, academic departments, and student services are all to be considered. . . . The individual must be viewed as a part of his social setting. Individual students are influenced by the attitudes and customs of their fellows. They react to their parents and to their teachers and reflect the mores of the community. A complete understanding of these students and a desirable modification of the educational program according to their needs can be achieved only when each student is considered in his broadest setting.[32]

Another report in the same series of the American Council on Education dealt in 1953 with the theme of *Students and Staff in a Social Context*. Its thesis is summarized in the statement:

Education in a social context means more than the organization of a modern curriculum, classroom discussion of contemporary problems, or the development of a program of common learnings—important as these refinements of traditional educational techniques may be. Edu-

[32] A. J. Brumbaugh and Ralph F. Berdie, *Student Personnel Programs in Transition* (Washington: American Council on Education, 1952), pp. 7–8.

cation in a social context implies more than a broadened use of the classroom, the laboratory, and the library; more than the reshuffling of old factual content; more than the addition of new subject matter. Education in a social context implies a realistic appraisal of the college as one among many methods of cultural induction and training. It also implies systematic use of the social structure and the group dynamics inherent in the college culture for the optimum development of students.[33]

In further explanation of the "personnel point of view" and as an indication of the methodology which may contribute to the fuller reintegration of college life, the report continues:

Scientific objectivity, historical perspective, and a vantage point from which campus life can be seen in relation to the larger culture are all a part of the ethnologist's point of view. His more specific tools involve close scrutiny of the folkways, mores, and other cultural patterns which emerge in campus life. These patterns are discovered through reading anecdotal materials as they appear in student themes, through listening to dormitory and campus conversations, through conducting informal interviews and group discussions, through examining campus newspapers and magazines, and through observing campus activities. . . . Just as an ethnologist would enter into the intimate life of a tribal society as a participant observer, so he tries in a modern group to catch its spirit, its taboos, its operating values, its patterns of interaction, its prestige symbols, and its class structure. Other tools include opinion surveys, attitude tests, guided interviews, projective techniques and related devices which social psychologists are developing to discover the undercurrents of feeling and judgment in individuals and among large groups of people. Best examples of these tools in use, unfortunately, do not come from campus life, where intuition is still relied upon more for administrative decisions than is research.[34]

Student Leadership

The personnel movement, then, along with sociological and anthropological analyses of campus life and with many of the academic "reforms" of recent decades, tends toward the rein-

[33] Robert L. Sutherland and others, *Students and Staff in a Social Context* (Washington: American Council on Education, 1953), p. 2.
[34] *Ibid.*, p. 21.

tegration of campus and classroom. A fourth tendency in the same direction lies in certain developments among students themselves. Students, as well as faculty members, have in recent years sought a greater degree of balance and focus in their college life. One of the major academic influences arising from the depression and World War II has been an increased maturity, a more serious outlook, on the part of students.

Many of the student activities to be dealt with more fully in later pages of this book illustrate the increasingly mature concern with college life felt by students. A share of the vitality which had prompted colonial student riots or led to the rise of organized athletics or found expression in college pranks has always been given to intellectual and artistic matters, and that share has increased in recent decades. Student clubs and societies, particularly since the 1930's, have concerned themselves with "causes" thought to have social significance. The movements for student government, encouraged by Lowell at Harvard and by Jordan at Stanford as a part of higher education took form all over the country. Through student government, students began to come to grips with some of the disorganization and distortion in college life.

At first, something apart and often at odds with administrative policy and practice, student government gradually grew into student *participation* in government. The student centers, already referred to, provided a unique educational resource, tending to improve and mature campus life. By the 1950's various earlier student groups had developed into the National Student Association, concerned with many aspects of college life and carrying on an educational program of its own. Even though student activities continue to be "a confusion of valuable and valueless interests" in many colleges, concern with what may be regarded as valuable from the point of view of higher education seems on the increase. More evidence on this matter may be found in later chapters of this volume.

Reintegration of College Life

The historical developments sketched in preceding pages indicate that, under the impulse of changes inherent in American social and educational development, we have passed through the collegiate way of life as discerned and defended by Cotton Mather, through decades in which student life was often at war with the intellectual concerns of the college, through an excessive separation of curriculum and extracurriculum, and are now moving toward the concept of an integrated college. In this integrated college the campus and classroom, for good or ill, are bound together. The curriculum seems certain to become less remote from the students and the extracurriculum less remote from the faculty. Current reassessments of higher education, as well as the increased maturity and sense of responsibility in American life, tend toward an integrated college life as a better utilization of academic resources.

Out of the combination of interests and developments in higher education as an aspect of the total American scene is beginning to emerge a more adequate and realistic concept of the totality of college experience. The currently revitalized search for the modern meaning of a liberal education which has already altered the curriculum and modified the elective system by programs of general education; the analysis of the extracurriculum which began in the 1920's and has continued in synchronization with the development of the newer social sciences; the rise of the personnel movement and the evolution of the role of dean of students as one seeking to orchestrate the varied harmonies of college life; and the increasing maturity of students arising in part from the sobering influences of contemporary life —all of these movements converge in what is an era of creativity as well as of controversy in American higher education. In a sense, both the curriculum and the extracurriculum are, in these years, breaking through the barriers of established stereotypes. Or, to put it in another way, philosophical interest in the meaning of higher education, psychological interest in the realistic cultivation of the worth of individual students, and sociological analysis of the mores and folkways of American college life have all led to a new and highly significant concept of higher education as an enculturation process shaped by the realities of American life.

Of primary importance is the application of a point of view toward the college community which is derived from the newer social sciences, particularly social psychology, sociology, and anthropology. It is in this point of view that the traditionally intellectual interests of those who emphasize what Hutchins calls the "higher learning" may find a meeting ground with the advocates of "education of the whole person." For it is an error to think of the curriculum as the one approach to the intellect and of the extracurriculum as the one approach to the emotions and values and vitalities of students. To see the student whole, and to see the life of a college whole, is to see the possibilities of developing campus "cultural environments which provide multiple opportunities for the development of students" in terms of their highest talents. With Valentine we may expect that

. . . a fully thought-out and well-rounded program of cultural and welfare activities will be found in the college of the future. . . . Some activities will be offered by the institutional authorities; some will be student sponsored; it is hoped that many will be cooperatively planned by joint student-faculty committees. The programs should serve dramatically to develop and elevate the minds and tastes of the students.[35]

College Life and the Higher Learning

The historical movements summarized in preceding pages as well as the recent influences tending toward reintegration of

[35] P. F. Valentine (ed.), *The American College* (New York: Philosophical Library, 1949), pp. 332–33.

college life are intimately related to the broad questions of purpose and function in higher education. American colleges and universities, for a variety of reasons rooted in our history, have always been much concerned with "education of the whole person," with the development of "well-rounded personalities," with the production of "good citizens," and with the development of "leaders" for all aspects of the national life. The citizenship motif and the vocational slant which arise from an intimate relationship between university and sustaining society have consistently been emphasized in American universities. Jefferson dwelt on them in his plans for the University of Virginia; Wayland spoke of them in his reforms at Brown in mid-century; they animated Eliot and Jordan. The 1945 report of a Harvard Committee on *General Education in a Free Society* reiterated that "education must look to the whole man"—"the good man, the good citizen, and the useful man." [36] They took form in the reports in 1947 and 1948 of the President's Commission on Higher Education. [37]

In a good deal of present-day commentary on higher education in the United States there is a tendency to equate the nonintellectual—some would say the anti-intellectual—purposes of college and university with student life, "strenuous activity," extracurricular interests. Just as some of the values of student life—some of the prestige given to the extracurriculum at the expense of the curriculum—were justified by observers of higher education at the turn of the century in terms of the contribution of such activities to "well-rounded development of leaders," so in the present years the same activities are blamed and criticized for the nonintellectual characteristics of higher education.

The most ardent of those critics who accuse higher education of having deserted the ancient intellectual purpose for which

[36] *General Education in a Free Society*, Report of the Harvard Committee (Cambridge: Harvard University Press, 1945), p. 74.

[37] President's Commission on Higher Education, *Higher Education for American Democracy* (Washington: Government Printing Office, 1947).

universities were founded frequently deride the concept of the college as a community. They make the same mistake that an early generation made of equating college life with student life. In reaction against the dichotomy of curriculum and extracurriculum they would throw out the latter. But as has already been suggested, the extracurriculum may have its own approach to intelligence and the cultivation of mind as well as feeling.

Present-day concepts of the nature of intelligence and of the intellectual life provide a substantial argument for the integration of curricular and extracurricular forces in higher education. We have departed steadily through several centuries of educational development from concepts of a sterile intellectualism, rigidly structured in artery-hardened disciplines. We have learned that newer fields of scholarly interest may embody strict standards of clear thinking fully as productively as may the traditional classics, and that all disciplines, new and old, may be living influences on the cultivation of intelligence or may be inert bodies of subject matter, depending on the situation in which they are encountered. We have learned that emotional health, physical well-being, character, citizenship, conduct, and vocation cannot be divorced from intelligence and that intelligence cannot be divorced from these other aspects of the person. To seek an integrated college life is not anti-intellectual in a modern and realistic sense, though it may do violence to traditional and particular patterns of intellectuality.

Sober analysis of purposes and means of achieving them recognizes the basic need for more effective cultivation of intelligence in the processes of higher education at this stage of American development and the necessity for seeking that end through the whole college way of life rather than through the curriculum alone. To proceed otherwise is to intensify an outworn separation in higher education. The Harvard Committee, emphasizing that general education must constantly aim at "effective thinking, communication, the making of relevant judgments, and the discrimination of values," points out that:

The aim of liberal education is the development of the whole man; and human nature involves instincts and sentiments as well as the intellect. Two dangers must be mentioned. First, there is the danger of identifying intelligence with the qualities of the so-called intellectual type—with bookishness and skill in the manipulation of concepts. We have tried to guard against this mistake by stressing the traits of relevant judgment and discrimination of values in effective thinking. Second, we must remember that intelligence, even when taken in its widest sense, does not exhaust the total potentialities of human nature. Man is not a contemplative being alone. Why is it, then, that education is conceived as primarily an intellectual enterprise when, in fact, human nature is so complex? For instance, man has his emotions and his drives and his will; why should education center on his intellect? The answer is found in the truth that *intelligence is not a special function* (or not that only) *but a way in which all human powers may function.* Intelligence is that leaven of awareness and reflection which, operating upon the native powers of men, raises them from the animal level and makes them truly human. *By reason we mean, not an activity apart, but rational guidance of all human activity. Thus the fruit of education is intelligence in action. The aim is mastery of life; and since living is an art, wisdom is the indispensable means to this end* [italics added].[38]

The point to be emphasized is that those who stress intellectual growth as the primary goal of higher education and those who stress character growth as a goal will alike gain from a valid reintegration in college life. Intelligence is not a negation of collegiate life, but, when that collegiate life is at its best, is a quality of it. The way to raise the intellectual level of the college is to develop collegiate mores which accord "beauties of the mind and spirit" high prestige. That is what Aydelotte sought at Swarthmore; it is one element in what Hutchins, without so much success, sought at Chicago. And the best of the student activities seek a form of "wisdom in action." To seek to create a collegiate community in which that end is paramount is no low or unworthy goal.

In the United States today there is wide concern over the meaning and realization of liberal education, a concern which

[38] *Op. cit.*, pp. 74–75.

animates faculty committees now at work in the smaller liberal arts colleges, in the general education programs of larger universities, and in the leading institutes of technology. Virtually all the plans and programs for the reincarnation of liberal learning which emerge from these committees concentrate on curriculum reform alone. But the creation of new courses or the juggling of course requirements will not alone bring to realization the higher learning. The setting in which courses operate as well as the values and concepts which students bring to them are of consequence. A liberal arts program which breaks down barriers between curriculum and extracurriculum is on a more substantial foundation by so doing. General education in the free society of Harvard, for example, must go hand in hand with the house plan of Lowell and the traditions of the Harvard Student Council—and even the jibes of the *Lampoon*—in order to be effective.

Can the ideal of a collegiate way of life which gives learning higher priority than it gives football, which makes the student center as much a house of thought and aesthetics as a house of play, be realized under modern conditions? A substantial obstacle perhaps is the inertia of faculties, a certain cloistered escapism on the part of some who are advocates of the bookish version of intellectuality. To see the college whole is, by the ordinary faculty member, left to the president and the dean of students. In a number of institutions joint faculty-student committees exist, but they are too generally concerned with minutiae. The motivating and girding of the college personnel itself for a real effort at constructive creation of a way of life harmonious with the academic functions in society, is the first requisite for development of the envisaged academic community.

It is often said by critics of higher education, particularly by critics whose orientation is toward the European tradition, that American colleges and universities cannot become adequately intellectualized until they are more restrictive. American campuses receive numbers of young people whose interest in things intellectual is not very high. They come in part because of the glamour of college life as derived from the public's concept of student activities and from a general conviction of the vocational value of college training. They are often suffering from a delusion as to what college life should be, and the reluctance of many college faculties to deal with that life, except as disciplinary situations arise, only perpetuates the delusion. Ordinarily the students now in college do not live up to the intellectual level of which they are capable. To challenge students more strictly and consistently on intellectual and aesthetic standards not alone in course requirements but also in the realms of campus tradition and behavior is significant for their education, for the integrity of the college, and for the role of higher education in our society.

It is doubtless true that the selective procedures for admission to college should be improved; not only do we need to see that those who come to higher education are qualified, but in the light of manpower needs, we need to make sure that all who are qualified do come. It is not likely, in any except a few atypical institutions, that colleges and universities will be in the future smaller than they are now. Indeed, the predictions for the immediate future indicate not only vastly larger numbers of students but also an increased percentage of the total college-age population actually in institutions of higher education. Research seems to indicate that expansion of opportunities in higher education will not lower the level of intelligence of the student body. It is of the greatest importance that the coming wave of students know they are entering institutions with high intellectual standards which are sustained by the campus mores. A contribution can be made to the problem of selecting students of quality by creating a college community, a collegiate way of life, which is particularly attractive to abler faculty members and abler students and less attractive to those who now seek admission into what they perhaps honestly but mistakenly regard as an academic combination of country club and marriage mart.

College Life in Modern America

The problem of size as affecting its character is a perplexing one for a college community, as for any other community. Certainly campus life is more easily susceptible to systematic development where there are relatively few people, but the campus life of a larger institution may be more varied, rich, and stimulating. The difference between the small and the large institution is the difference between the town and the metropolis. Each has its distinctive assets, problems, characteristic processes of behavior and change. In neither of them can the "way of life" be ruled out as unimportant or as necessarily anti-intellectual.

Size and character of an institution are intimately related to the respective merits and demerits of rural and urban institutions of higher education. The rural college is a distinctively American type of institution. In many cases the once-rural college has been engulfed by the city, as Cambridge has environed Harvard, and New Haven, Yale. Many of the more recently established institutions, such as the University of Chicago, the College of the City of New York, Tulane University, Boston University, have been urban from their founding. In most American cities may be found institutions of higher education where the dividing line between campus and city is difficult to discern.

Williams in Massachusetts, Oberlin in Ohio, and Carleton in Minnesota, for example, are well-defined communities within themselves. So also are the state colleges which are widely distributed over the United States, extending from Trenton to

Santa Barbara. Most students live on campus; the colleges are residential in the fullest degree. New York University, on the other hand, has few student residence facilities; as a commuters' college, its life follows different patterns; it is susceptible to different influences and pressures; it has different and highly metropolitan problems and challenges. The character of college life in such urban institutions has not been so carefully analyzed nor so nostalgically recorded in literature as has the life of the relatively rural college, but its life is nevertheless structured and its traditions and mores are certainly influential on its members. So also is the life at an institution like Ball State Teachers College in Muncie, Indiana, in which the commuter pattern is perhaps more typical of the whole country than is that of Williams or New York University. With almost three thousand students, Ball State draws approximately a third of them each day from the homes of Muncie itself. A second third also live at home, but in a rural hinterland which, in a motor age, radiates from the campus for more than fifty commuter miles. Only a third of the students are residents in college houses, a typical proportion in that the colleges of the country as a whole have housing facilities for not more than a third of the total group of students now enrolled.

College life, in the sociological and comprehensive sense presented in these pages, is not exclusive to a residential institution or a commuters' institution, to a rural or an urban center of learning, to a large or a small institution. The college way of life has distinctive flavor for those who are in it physically for twenty-four hours a day and for those whose physical presence on campus is limited to a few hours each day. The patterns of value and action, the modes and moods of thought, the relations among commuters and dormitory residents and those who dwell in fraternities and sororities are elements in the structure of the college community. A realistic approach to analysis of college life starts with the actualities of existence there; for that analysis a preconceived assumption of the necessity for an isolated, residential college alone is no more justified than would be the analysis of urban and suburban America in terms of America's traditional small towns. The collegiate way of life in contemporary America is by no means identical with the collegiate way of life in earlier decades, nostalgia to the contrary. There are wide divergencies in college life within our extraordinary variety of institutions of higher education. But in each institution there is a way of life—a tradition, a set of values, a pattern of mores—which is the conditioning environment, the characteristic influence, and the framework of educative experience for the members of the college.

The thesis which has been advanced in this discussion, and supported by reference to historical developments and to current analyses of American higher education, is that the curriculum and the extracurriculum need to be further integrated if we are to achieve the distinctive kind of higher education America seeks. It has been here argued that college education arises from the whole of college living. It has been suggested that, in an earlier day, the various facets of collegiate life were relatively unified, though rigidity of control by the masters and adherence to a Puritan orthodoxy led to breakdown of this earlier, rather formalized integration. During the last century the college was bifurcated, but in recent decades the peak of the resultant disharmony seems to have been passed. There are hopeful signs on hand that higher education in this country has already passed through the worst of the excesses of a student life which had little to do with the basic purposes of higher education. Substantial efforts are now under way for bringing the main show and the side shows, to use Woodrow Wilson's simile, into one tent. There are at hand many of the resources and motivations for creating, consciously and imaginatively, a collegiate way of life which is exciting and challenging for those who share in it, and which has its focus on the intellectual and aesthetic concerns which are the college's main business. This can be done by avoiding both the extremes of a bookish intellectualism and of an escapist and juvenile activism.

It follows that the analysts and directors of higher education need, particularly in this era, to see the college whole. Reference has already been made to the urgency of conceiving liberal education in terms wider than courses and curricular patterns. By the same token the athletic program needs consideration in terms wider than intercollegiate competition and sports page publicity. We can profit from analysis of the relationship between drama clubs and drama classes, between classes in writing and activities in student publications, between classes in political science and student participation in government. Those who study the nature and effectiveness of any one specific goal or interest in higher education must deal with college as a whole. Those who analyze the degree to which we are making students economically literate, or sensitizing them to the beauties of painting and music, or developing in them responsible citizenship, or ability at honest expression in the English language, or ability at reflective thinking, or stalwartness in intellectual integrity must alike examine both the curriculum and the extracurriculum.

College Life and World Affairs

Succeeding chapters of the present volume are concerned with education about world affairs, a phase of education having no little consequence in the situation in which the United States exists today. As has been indicated in the Foreword, this volume is one of a series, each of which examines a particular facet of higher education's resources and activities bearing on the conduct of world affairs. The present volume will deal with the out-of-class, relatively informal aspects of American college life. If the thesis advanced in preceding pages be true, this phase of college life has marked influence in the collegiate preparation of Americans for the role in world affairs which time and tide in the affairs of men and nations have cast upon them. But the volume deals with these phases of collegiate life not in a separatist sense; it emphasizes the unified framework which has been described in preceding pages.

While the following chapters deal with "members of the college," cocurricular activities, and the student habitat, all within the framework of concern with education about world affairs, they are not presented as matters having greater consequence than the curriculum, which is treated in another volume. In terms of the basic conceptualizations which have been outlined in the first chapter of this volume, the topics of succeeding chapters are presented as interrelated parts, though often neglected aspects of the whole of college life. They are parts which need to be envisaged as in partnership rather than in conflict with other more formal and more official parts of college life. The chapters are presented, not in a partisan defense of the extracurriculum but as a survey of resources at hand for the integration of college life in terms of the thesis of American higher education which is embodied in this introductory chapter as it comes to focus on the topic of education about world affairs. The philosophy was well expressed in his inaugural address at the University of Minnesota by Lotus D. Coffman:

A university is not an aggregation of individuals merely; it has its social mind, to which every individual contributes. The social mind of a university is not lifeless and inert; it is a powerful dynamic touching the life of faculty and students at every turn. . . . The development of a genuinely wholesome institutionality through the personnel of a high-minded faculty and the associated life of students and faculty in classrooms, libraries, laboratories, commons, union buildings, auditoriums, and stadiums is the supremely important problem of a modern university.

. . . .

There are certain ideals, there is a certain tone, there is a certain atmosphere characterizing the life of a university that distinguishes it from every other human institution. Whatever these ideals, that tone or atmosphere, may be, it is as truly a function of the university to foster, conserve, safeguard, and stimulate them as it is a function of the university to provide instruction of a specific and definite character. Both make their impacts upon the student. [39]

In the end, by considering the extracurriculum in its practical relationship to the function of higher education, we may come to achieve the university as Whitehead saw it in 1929:

The justification for a university is that it preserves the connection between knowledge and the zest of life, by uniting the young and the old in the imaginative consideration of learning. The university imparts information, but it imparts it imaginatively. . . . This atmosphere of excitement . . . transforms knowledge. A fact is no longer a bare fact; it is invested with all its possibilities. It is no longer a burden on the memory; it is energizing as the poet of our dreams, and as the architect of our purposes. [40]

It is this concept of a university as a community to which this volume is devoted. Without attention to it, the problem and challenges of education about world affairs cannot be dealt with in adequate terms. College life itself may contribute effectively to the education about foreign relations and international affairs which is demanded by the age in which today's students live.

[39] Coffman, *The State University: Its Work and Problems* (Minneapolis: University of Minnesota Press, 1934), pp. 10–11, 18–19.
[40] Alfred North Whitehead, *The Aims of Education and Other Essays* (New York: Macmillan Co., 1929), p. 139.

———————————CHAPTER TWO

Facilities for Informal Education
about World Affairs

A college . . . is a place where all the facilities for acquiring a well-rounded education are conveniently assembled. A few yards away in this direction is a library, in that direction a laboratory; equally convenient are a gymnasium and a chapel and places where one may see good pictures and hear good music and experiment with a piano. Scattered about are teachers expounding their lore and offering to open vistas into one or another field of learning. But I suddenly realize that I must add one important phrase to my definition: a place where the facilities for acquiring an education are conveniently assembled in an atmosphere conducive to study.—Burges Johnson, Campus versus Classroom

ENORMOUS emotionalism is attached even to the physical structure of an American college campus. Students and alumni and faculty refer fondly to Old Nassau, the Rotunda, Old Beecher, the Old Capitol at Iowa, the six stark and beautiful columns on the Missouri campus. Someone once defined a college as "any building with ivy on it," and there are certainly such buildings in the nostalgic memories of most graduates of American colleges. In *Which Way Parnassus?* Percy Marks wrote:

A college . . . is a creator of a sentiment that is very precious. To ignore that sentiment is to ignore the soul of the college. The senti-

36

ment—or, if you will, sentimentality—comes from many sources, but it is more real in many ways than any number of trustees, presidents or deans; it is lasting, and it is significant. Much of it, I think, comes from the college's physical self, and most colleges are in some way lovely. No one has a right to talk about the University of California who hasn't strolled under the oaks in springtime. Many of us learned more from the beauty of the campus than we ever learned in the classroom, and anyone who neglects that beauty neglects something so vital to us that we cannot listen to his words with patience. Who can talk wisely of Yale who hasn't seen the wonder of the Harkness Memorial? . . . Dartmouth can never quite fail so long as it is surrounded by the New Hampshire hills, and Dartmouth Row gleams white behind the elms.[1]

The beauty of many revered academic places and vistas must assuredly contribute to the motivations and aspirations of succeeding generations of students. These emotion-packed elements in the college environment are a part of the aesthetic and attitudinal education of students. When, among them, are such items as the lovely stone lanterns, gift of Japanese alumni, on the Harvard Yard and on the campus at Berkeley, or the Trojan pillar, gift of Turkish alumni at the University of Southern California, or even the architectural forms borrowed from other cultures, the sentiment of devotion to alma mater may include some sense of the unity of man's civilization and of the brotherhood of man. It is surprising, considering the interest of academic people in world affairs, the international contacts and services of academic personnel, and the number of foreign alumni, that there are so few such monuments to international bonds on American campuses. The brick colonial-style building contributed by Amherst men to Doshisha University in Japan symbolizes the United States for many Japanese. American University in Beirut gains force as a transplanted American campus. The architecture of the Cité Universitaire in Paris, with buildings contributed in the typical styles of many lands, is itself a strong and visible influence on the Cité's international character.

[1] Marks, *Which Way Parnassus?* (New York: Harcourt, Brace & Co., 1926), pp. 7–8.

American colleges could profit by the further development of striking symbols of other cultures in their campus designs.

While it is important to recognize the aesthetic qualities cultivated by this setting in which college life is lived, it would be ridiculous to suggest that a generously constructed college plant guarantees a good college education or even that a good college education is impossible in an inadequate plant. It is equally false to assume that aesthetic surroundings invariably cultivate in students the higher qualities of value, of integrity, of sensitivity and humaneness, which are essential to a mature and farsighted outlook on the world. It would be foolish to rest the program of education about world affairs on the physical adornments of college life, no matter how great their emotional and aesthetic impact. But at the same time, all the American experience in higher education attests the importance of the campus environment to the kind of "well-rounded" higher education Americans think most desirable. The environment influences the students' sense of the universal and the true. The spirit generated by the place cannot be ignored in realistic analysis of educational programs, including education about world outlook.

There are distinctive physical features other than classrooms and laboratories on the American academic landscape which are central to the character and operation of an educative college life such as is described in this volume. Some of these physical facilities are intimately related to education about world affairs. In terms of Burges Johnson's definition of a college, quoted above, there are on every campus "facilities for learning" about foreign policy, world affairs, and cultural interrelations which must be considered by any institution which is determined to make maximum contribution to education of its members in this area. The library, the college union, the chapel, the housing arrangements must be utilized along with the classroom and laboratory if the job of educating about world affairs is to

be done effectively. It is to the functions of these agencies—
these relatively informal, out-of-class always educative-for-good-
or-for-bad influences on the campus—that this chapter is devoted.

International Houses

There are, of course, campus buildings which in their established functions have a primary relationship to matters international. These buildings have at least an indirect influence on
the whole campus, and sometimes a direct and powerful influence on large numbers of the students. The International
Houses at Berkeley and Chicago and New York are institutions
of this character.

The first of these monumental houses was opened in New
York City in 1924, gift of John D. Rockefeller and a tribute to
the long-expressed friendly concern for foreign students of Mr.
and Mrs. Harry Edmonds. As far back as 1910 Mr. Edmonds
by chance encountered a lonely Chinese student and through
him became interested in the large number of such lonely student visitors in the New York area. Sunday evening suppers
for foreign visitors, at first in the Edmonds' home and later in a
hall of Columbia University, led to the organization of an Intercollegiate Cosmopolitan Club. It was the work of this club
in facilitating contacts of student visitors and student hosts that
attracted Mr. Rockefeller's attention and philanthropy. The
house in New York proved so successful that, after careful survey, similar centers were built by Mr. Rockefeller in Berkeley
in 1930 and in Chicago in 1932.[2] A fourth house, familiar to
many American students in France, is located at the Cité Universitaire, the program center of a group of nationality dormi-

[2] See Kathryn Close, "That Brotherhood May Prevail: The Story of the
International House Idea" (Reprinted from the *International House Quar-
terly,* Autumn 1944, revised April 1952; New York: International House
Association, 1952).

tories erected by some thirty countries for their nationals studying in Paris.

The three American houses are partly dormitories, partly club houses for members both resident and nonresident, partly social and recreational centers, and, particularly in recent years, educational centers with informal programs bearing on cultural characteristics, international relations, and world affairs. In addition to providing centers for the reception of foreign students, for the meeting of foreign and American students and faculty, and for programs and activities of international interest, the very existence of the houses or international centers has an influence on campus interests and mores. Even students who never use the facilities of the houses are at least reminded of the international flavor of the universities by seeing the houses as part of the campus. This is particularly true at Berkeley and Chicago where the International Houses have a more intimate and obvious relation to the physical campus than has the house in New York City.

Constructed under the early impact of the great rush of foreign students to American institutions, these International Houses and centers have served a great human need and to a less-well-appraised extent a major educational need. They have both served high purposes and revealed some of the complex problems of intercultural relations among academic people. The danger has become evident of peopling the houses almost exclusively with foreign students; in the pressure of caring for many foreign students, the houses for a period were almost agencies of cultural isolation rather than of contact between American and foreign students. So far as their residential operations are concerned, they have now adopted quota systems governing the proportions of Americans and foreigners resident in each house.

One of the problems of integrating the International Houses into campus life is their structural organization as semiautonomous agencies related to the university. Each house has its own Board of Governors; the New York house, and to a limited extent the others also, serve more than one university. The house board and the university authorities on occasion pursue differing policies, or at least fail to coordinate effectively on such matters. As a result of this and other factors there is a tendency today to develop smaller, often nonresidential, international houses within the full control of college or university. It seems unlikely that additional centers in the model of these three great pioneering institutions will be constructed.

One outgrowth of the houses during the last decade has been the development of an alumni association, the International House Association. Some sixty thousand persons, scattered all over the world, who have been at some time residents in one of the houses, are organized in eighty-two chapters. The association publishes a quarterly journal and a news sheet for members, and a headquarters staff encourages program activities. In particular, November 10 is celebrated by many chapters as International House Day. Such celebrations are not only occasions for alumni festivity but also for reviving contacts with friends in other lands and for studying, through lectures and discussions, significant international developments.

In addition to the great houses in New York, Chicago, and Berkeley, smaller clubs or residences for foreign students have been established on many campuses. The International Center on the campus at Fisk University—providing a reception center for foreign students, facilities for holding meetings and concerts and for arranging exhibits, and with a program to stimulate campus interest in world affairs—is a worthy example of these houses. The Fisk University self-survey on education in international relations reports that:

The Center provides a focus of stimulation for thinking along international lines, whether in politics, economics, history, sociology, music, art, philosophy, or literature. To this purpose the Center offers a varied program of lectures by men and women prominent in international affairs, panel discussions on current world problems, foreign feature and documentary films, international dinners, art exhibits, music, and play readings. The Center welcomes students visiting here from other countries and assists them in adjusting to life in a new atmosphere. The Center is also open during the day to students for informal conversation, for listening to music, and for reading the foreign and American newspapers and magazines and current books to which the Center subscribes.[3]

At Indiana University, as at many other institutions, a social center is maintained for groups interested in promoting international relations. Facilities, including a kitchen, a dining room, and living rooms are available for meals and parties, where foreign students can entertain friends. International House at the State University of Iowa is "non-residential and quite small." The self-survey report from Iowa describes its work as follows:

In addition to its general aim of affording a "home" rather than a residence for foreign students and their American friends, it sponsors a variety of programs directed toward human understanding rather than intellectual knowledge of the way other people live. The House may be reserved by all the students of one nation for the purpose of holding a religious or cultural festival peculiar to them, and to which they invariably invite their American friends. It stages exhibitions of craft work, clothing, and art from geographic areas. Its criticism of its own program is typical of such institutions: too few American students make use of it.[4]

A difficulty encountered by most of the houses and centers affects their social and recreational and educational as well as their residential aspects. This is the problem of cultivating for foreign students contacts with Americans who are really representative of American student bodies. In situations where

---

[3] "Report on Fisk University and World Affairs," *Universities and World Affairs,* Document No. 74 (Mimeographed; New York: Carnegie Endowment for International Peace, 1955), p. 8.

[4] "The State University of Iowa and World Affairs," *Universities and World Affairs,* Document No. 80 (Mimeographed; New York: Carnegie Endowment for International Peace, 1955), pp. 95–96.

foreign students are regarded as cultural novelties, there has been some tendency for American students who had failed to establish satisfying personal relationships and prestige with their own group to cultivate the foreign group as a means of ego satisfaction. The task of bringing a cross section of the American student body into the dormitories and dining rooms and program activities of the international houses and centers is of major importance. In this task, the relationship of the international house or international center to other social centers on the campus becomes basic. If the international house or center is so located, constructed, and operated that it serves the function of a general student union, the problem is readily solved. Or if the foreign student center is a wing of the student union building, as at Michigan, the situation is relatively favorable. But if the international house is located on the periphery of campus life, or in competition with other social centers, or lacks conveniences for its effective operation, or lacks discerning and sensitive leadership, its role as a center for intercultural contact and understanding is not very substantial. One can find too many instances where an international house, more or less blessed by the college, is an isolated pocket of campus life, violating the very purposes for which it was created.

Nationality Houses and Rooms

Another kind of house, found on many campuses, serves a related function and aptly illustrates an advantageous relationship between the curriculum and the extracurriculum. This is the foreign nationality house, designed primarily as a center for informal language study and for contact with the culture of a particular nation. Italian House at Columbia University, the French House at Mills, and the Latin American House of the Louisiana State University illustrate these campus developments. The University of Washington, for example, maintains each summer quarter a French House, Spanish House, and Russian House which provide some of the linguistic advantages of actually living abroad for a month or two.

These nationality houses have contributed substantially to the development of language instruction, to the planned use of college life for educative ends, and to the study of the national areas with which they deal. In a sense, the nationality houses are informal precursors of the world-area study centers which have become important in the formal curriculum of higher education in recent years. However, if the nationality houses are operated purely as adjuncts to the language and humanities curriculum, or if they are run simply as social centers, a place for novelty-seeking tourists-at-home, they lose their effectiveness. They are then retreats either from campus life or from intellectual respectability. They seem most successful where developed under leadership which is sensitive both to academic demands and to informal human relations, and where they are accorded real prestige alike by the faculty and by the general student body.

One of the most interesting and dramatic developments in the creation of a university environment reflecting a variety of national cultures is found in the unique nationality rooms of the University of Pittsburgh. In 1927 a desire of the university to cultivate closer ties with the nationality groups resident in the cosmopolitan area of Pittsburgh led to the establishment of Nationality Committees in the community, each of which became interested in designing and decorating and furnishing a room in the university's new "skyscraper" Cathedral of Learning. Since that time eighteen rooms have been established reflecting the spirit and art of the Chinese, Czechoslovakian, English, French, German, Greek, Hungarian, Italian, Irish, Lithuanian, Norwegian, Polish, Romanian, Russian, Scottish, Swedish, Syrian-Lebanese, and Yugoslav cultures. The rooms themselves are of striking beauty. The black, red, and gold of the Chinese Room, the panels of the English Room made of wood from the bombed House of Commons; the magnificent stained glass fairy-tale windows of the German Room and the window panels of the Hungarian Room; the Paderewski manuscripts in their special cabinet in the Polish Room; the tapestries and panels and paintings of the various Slavic rooms; and the tables and chairs in appropriate styles for each of the rooms create a major cultural resource for the university. Among the gifts made to the rooms have been a Charles IV brocade given by Czechoslovakia in 1948, a set of tea tables from Queen Mary, a fireback cast in 1588 to commemorate the defeat of the Armada, a seventeenth-century portrait of the first woman to receive a doctorate from Padova, and ikons of Old Russia. In a number of cases the rooms were decorated by outstanding artists from the country involved. And in every case the Nationality Committee of the Pittsburgh area took great care and pride in making the room into a fit reflection of the best of the culture from its homeland.

The important factor is not alone that the rooms were created but that they are part of the regular working of the university. A special organization of women students, the Nationality Rooms Hostesses, study the rooms, guide visitors through them, and participate in social and cultural events sponsored from time to time in the rooms by the off-campus Nationality Committees. And the rooms are also in regular use as classrooms. In 1954 the Greek Room housed classes in modern Greek, the classics, history, and speech; the German Room was the meeting place for classes in German, English, French, and insurance. Student meetings are held in the rooms; they are the setting of formal receptions, special lectures, the granting of awards.

It should be recorded, too, that the impetus which led Nationality Committees to sponsor and create these rooms carried beyond the rooms themselves. A general Council of the Nationality Rooms Committees has sponsored a series of lectures, in

English, on the literature of the countries represented. The committees contribute to the funds for exchange of students and provide awards to help particularly worthy students travel abroad. The Norwegian Committee has, on several occasions, sent students or instructors for a summer of study in Norway. The Slavic Committees have aided in bringing a specialist to the university to plan the development of a systematic program in Slavonic studies. The Nationality Committees are not only significant agencies for cooperation between the university and the metropolitan area of Pittsburgh, not only donors of a unique resource in the university's physical environment, but they are also significant in enabling Pittsburgh students and faculty to become more familiar with the national cultures of the modern world.

College Unions

The rise of college unions as characteristic structures on the American campus symbolizes in some respects the integrated college life toward which American higher education seems to be moving. The beginnings of the union movement go well back into academic history; the debating groups which took the form of the Cambridge Union in 1815 and the Oxford Union in 1823 were very early influential on the American side of the Atlantic. So also was the Glasgow Union, one of whose founders was later active in the academic life of the University of Michigan. By 1832 a debating society known as the Union existed at Harvard. After a decade it lapsed, only to reappear in the 1890's, with more emphasis on its social than on its argumentative function. By 1901 a building was constructed in Cambridge to house the recreated Harvard Union.

During the 1890's there was also agitation among students at the University of Pennsylvania for a building to serve them as a club house. Here the desire to house in one central location the offices of various student organizations was a major influence, and as early as 1896 led to the construction of Howard Houston Hall. As Edward Cheyney wrote in 1901:

When completed it proved to be the most beautiful and artistic building in the University, with every appointment of good taste and convenience and suited to a great variety of student uses. It contains a swimming pool and baths, gymnasium, bowling alleys, billiard, pool and chess tables, lunch counters and facilities for more extensive repasts, reading and writing rooms, an auditorium and smaller rooms for religious services, and a large number of separate rooms for the use of committees, the Athletic Association, the Young Men's Christian Association, for the college papers, for the musical clubs, and a dark room for photography. . . . Student self-government was applied by putting it under the immediate charge of a House Committee composed of students, with one member of the faculty, and in case of need an ultimate right of veto at the hands of a Board of Directors consisting of the Deans of the various faculties. For the enjoyment of its facilities the Houston Club was formed, by which students and alumni could at a small cost obtain its use and the running expenses could be provided for. Since its opening it has been used by averages varying from 1000 to 1500 persons a day during the whole of term time. The influence of Houston Hall over the physical, mental, and moral life of the students has been most beneficent. Few if any gifts to colleges have exerted a more varied or more continuous influence for good.[5]

In addition to the union buildings at Pennsylvania and at Harvard, two other unions were constructed before World War I. In 1903 Faunce Hall was built at Brown and in 1909 the Ohio Union was built at Columbus—the first such union built with public funds. During this first period in the establishment of unions the prevailing concept was that of a social center, a means for facilitating and centralizing the extracurricular student activities which had become so important a part of college life. Union organizations were gradually formed at many institutions; while many were without housing facilities at first, a crescendo of construction of union buildings came in the 1920's.

[5] From chapter by Cheyney in *Universities and Their Sons* (Boston, Mass.: R. Herndon Co., 1901), II, 173–74.

The Michigan Union, modeled under the influence of Hart House at the University of Toronto, was opened in 1920. The most impressive of the unions to that date, it signaled a great period of construction. By 1947 there were 150 union buildings on American campuses and at least as many more in the planning stage. After World War II there was a greater increase in union building than in any other type of campus construction. The unions are typically among the most attractive and most functionally designed buildings on American campuses and are uniquely characteristic of American colleges. Only in recent years have European centers of higher learning turned their attention to such student centers.

While American unions took their origin from the debating clubs of British universities, they were predominantly social institutions during the first half-century of their physical existence on American campuses. They were conceived as club houses, centers for recreational, leisure-time activity. But during recent years, and particularly since World War II, the unions have been increasingly planned and operated as educative centers, housing lectures, recitals, concerts, forums, discussion groups, exhibits, and institutes as well as dances and movies and the offices of student clubs, publications, and associations. The term "student union" has been outgrown even to the extent that it was ever applicable. The unions are used by faculty and alumni as well as by students and are almost always referred to as "college unions." Their purposes are now academic, intellectual, and aesthetic as well as recreational.

The fact that the college unions are ordinarily under the control of a board representing both students and faculty, and that their programs are jointly planned and administered and shared in by older and younger members of the college, gives them cocurricular character and strong vitality. The union has grown into a cultural center for campus life. It is not just a lounge for idle leisure nor a nerve center for the strenuous activities of which Canby wrote, but an institution with an educative mission. Jointly run by and for faculty and students, it is an institution with a concern for the enduring aesthetic, intellectual, and social satisfactions of educated men and women.

In a college union operated as a broadly educative center, the opportunities for instructing members of the college are many, and, systematically utilized, they may be important influences in collegiate education about world affairs. Perhaps most important, though least subject to systematization, are the personal contacts and friendships which are facilitated in the union as the "living room of the college." A visiting professor of philosophy at a Kansas college, for example, was particularly impressed with this possibility. Although he taught regular classes of his own and lectured frequently in other classes, he felt that the late afternoon hours he spent at the union with informal groups of students, drinking cokes when he wanted the customary tea, brought him into closer rapport with students, and provided his best opportunities both for teaching philosophy and for presenting his own national culture on the American campus.

Students frequently report, by questionnaire and in conversation, that informal contact at their unions with professors, foreign students, and others interested in world affairs have influenced their attitudes and added to their information and understanding. The lounges and browsing library, music rooms, and committee rooms, dining tables, and snack bars are resources for mutual contact among members of the university community. In them Cardinal Newman's concept of the university as a network of friendly, stimulating, and educative human relations becomes a reality. The ideal expressed in the Founders' Prayer for Hart House, the union of the University of Toronto, is not infrequently achieved on many campuses:

The prayer of the Founders is, that Hart House, under the guidance of its Warden, may serve, in the generations to come, the highest interests of this University by drawing into a common fellowship the members of the several colleges and faculties, and by gathering into a true society the teacher and the student, that the members of Hart House may discover within its walls the true education that is to be found in good fellowship, in friendly disputation and debate, in the conversation of wise and earnest men, in music, pictures and the play, in casual book, in sports and games and the mastery of the body. . . .[6]

Systematic programs of discussion groups, forums, lectures, exhibits, as well as recreational events, are increasingly a part of the college union operations. At the University of Buffalo, for example, the constitution and plan of the union recognize the importance of cultivating intellectual interests and specifically suggest, as regular phases of its program, lectures, discussion groups, forums, reading clubs, and educational exhibits. The Union of the University of Wisconsin is an outstanding illustration of the development of a cultural center, helping to bridge the gap between campus and classroom. In his inaugural address in 1904 President Van Hise referred to the "communal life of instructors and students in work, in play, and in social relations" as "the very essence of the spirit of Oxford and Cambridge." He then added:

If the University of Wisconsin is to do for the sons of the state what Oxford and Cambridge are doing for the sons of England, not only in producing scholars and investigators but in making men, it must once more have halls of residence and to these must be added a commons and Union.[7]

Van Hise worked with student leaders in the formation of a campus group, the Wisconsin Union, intended as a unifying social and cultural organization for all students. Later a member of the Board of Regents, Walter Kohler, Sr., picked up the

[6] Edith O. Humphreys, *College Unions: A Handbook on College Community Centers* (Ithaca, N.Y.: The Association of College Unions, 1946), p. 66.

[7] *Report on the Wisconsin Union,* prepared by the Memorial Union Building Committee in observance of the twenty-fifth anniversary of the Union Building in 1953 (Madison, Wis.: Memorial Union), p. 3.

Van Hise concept and organized a committee of alumni and friends to raise funds for a union building, and the building was opened in 1928. Enlarged on several occasions since then, the union is now one of the most imposing and one of the best-programed unions of the country.

The *Report on the Wisconsin Union,* already referred to, indicates that some 15,000 people use the union every day; its services and programs reach 95 percent of the student body, and an additional 5,200 alumni and townspeople. In 1951 more people—620,000—attended cultural programs of the union "than the combined attendance of all sports events put together, including football, basketball, and boxing." In 1951–52 there was an average of 26 events at the union each day. There were more than 600 students serving on active union committees, and these committees sponsored "149 different types of social, cultural, and recreational programs"—forums, student-faculty coffee hours, lectures, theatrical productions, art exhibitions, debates, ballets, creative writing contests, among them. The same report says:

Another pioneering enterprise has been to utilize the Union as a laboratory for teaching. Wisconsin is the first Union to be designated as an educational division of the university (the Division of Social Education). The Union was one of three departments instrumental in initiating a . . . major in Community Leadership. . . . In other directions the Union's teaching service includes giving part of the training course in institutional management for home economics students . . . and conducting the course in art museum administration, using the gallery as laboratory.[8]

The teaching services are symptomatic of a new relationship with education into which unions are now growing. In 1951–52 the Wisconsin Union was also host to almost 700 conferences and institutes arranged by faculty members or jointly by faculty and students. The union is a resource for the cultivation of learning which is uniquely appropriate to American higher edu-

[8] *Ibid.,* p. 11.

cation and which is more powerful than most institutions have yet realized.

A great many of the union activities have a direct relation to education about world affairs. The union provides a meeting place for foreign and American students and faculty members. Its endless bull sessions are in part focused on international problems and issues. Its art exhibits, theatrical productions, motion picture showings may, and do, deal maturely with cultures other than our own. At the Wisconsin Union programs of the last two years include: a debate with representatives of the Oxford Union on the relation of the welfare state to liberty; talks on their countries by the Ambassadors from Viet Nam and Great Britain; lectures by Justice Douglas on Southeast Asia, by the Director of the Imperial Institute in London on problems of West Africa, by Mrs. Roosevelt and by Trygve Lie on the United Nations, by Harold Stassen on American foreign policy; film showings on various nations; panel discussions by visiting professors on current international issues; and an annual festival and exposition staged by foreign students. Without considering such activities as these, there cannot be a realistic appraisal of education for world affairs at the University of Wisconsin. These union activities certainly reached many more students than did the classes in world affairs, and provided learning opportunities for students enrolled in these classes which could not be duplicated in courses alone. More systematic attention, at Wisconsin and elsewhere, on the part of the faculty members concerned with international relations to the further development of these activities and to their more effective coordination with course offerings is to be desired.

The shift in concept of a union from the "romantic period" of the 1920's when the irresponsibilities of student life were most extreme to the serious and systematic though informal and experimental educational concept now widely developing has, unfortunately, often been realized more keenly by students and union staffs than by faculty members. Reporting an extensive survey of the unions in 1946, Edith Humphreys commented:

> One would expect faculty members to make use of the educational potentialities of the union. The fact is, however, that the majority of faculty members have not recognized the union as an agency capable of complementing the work of the classroom. Such is the case even among many who conceive of the college as having a responsibility in developing not only academic intelligence but also what Malcolm McLean . . . terms social intelligence, practical intelligence, creative intelligence and appreciative intelligence.[9]

On many campuses today one gets the impression that many faculty members still think of the union as an escape valve for student energy; the union is still too frequently a student union rather than a college union, particularly where faculty clubs exist apart from the union building. But the trend toward joint faculty-student programing as well as joint faculty-student administration of the unions is very strong.

University Religious Centers

Other features of campus architecture which constitute a significant resource for education about world affairs are the buildings devoted to religion. On the campuses of most privately endowed institutions, the university church or chapel is a central structure on the campus. The great gothic chapels of Princeton and the University of Chicago, the white-spired chapels of the New England colleges, and the chapels created by sectarian founders all over the country symbolize a religious element close to the convictions and motivations of all men. Just off the campus of most publicly supported, nondenominational institutions are to be found religious centers for students which have been built and are maintained by denominations as services to students on the campus. At the State University of Iowa, at the University of Washington, at the University of

[9] Humphreys, *op. cit.*, p. 48.

Florida, to mention only three examples of what is common throughout the country, these religious centers have a considerable influence on student thought and are an intimate part of the college life. These centers maintain not only houses for worship but also facilities for discussion groups, lectures, concerts, special classes, and recreational events. Their leaders are ordinarily sensitive to the great issues of world affairs; religion has throughout history been concerned with such matters, and the revival in religious interests of the present generation gives increased influence to the programs of these university religious establishments.

In the religious services devoted to the application of moral tenets to human affairs, including international affairs; in the lectures provided, often by persons of wide international experience and outlook; in the organized discussion groups; in the consideration of missionary movements; in far-flung philanthropies; and in the recreational and social endeavors of these religious centers many students are made both to think and to feel about the nature and morality of human relations, about foreign policies, cultural contacts, and world affairs. An observer at one large state university in the Middle West rates the lectures and discussion groups regularly scheduled at the just-off-campus religious centers as the most influential, nonformal elements of college life in shaping students' attitudes about world affairs. At the University of California at Los Angeles the off-campus University Religious Center maintained cooperatively by various denominations is a powerful factor in all campus life, touching student politics, organizing student travel abroad, and helping to shape the ideas and outlooks of many students. The programs of the centers maintained widely by the Society of Friends, as well as their summer institutes and international work camps, are continuously concerned with good human relations on the international level. The work of the Newman Clubs, of the Hillel Foundation, and of such religiously motivated lay organizations as the National Conference of Christians and Jews has an increasing influence in college. The Young Men's and Young Women's Christian Associations, long active in international humanitarian and cultural movements, continue to be centers for study groups, lectures, and forums bearing on world affairs.

The deep concern of all religious groups with moral and spiritual values as applied to the brotherhood of man makes these groups a potent educative influence. Realistic appraisal of what is done to educate American students in world outlook must include these religiously motivated activities. They are not activities which can be systematically coordinated on a campus, nor are they subject to easy measurement and evaluation. They warrant, however, more attention and support from specialists in international relations and from specialists in the educational process than they ordinarily receive.

The College Library

Central in the architectural design of virtually all institutions of higher education is the college or university library; the library structure, often of beauty as well as utility, is an outstanding feature of the campus landscape. While the traditional function of the library is that of collecting, housing, and distributing books, that is, of servicing the instructional and research programs of the university, it has also come to have in recent decades significant independent educational functions of its own. It is but commonplace now to assert that "the library must play a positive rather than merely passive role in university education."

In connection with the Carnegie Endowment program on universities and world affairs, a letter of inquiry was sent to the librarians in 96 widely distributed, representative colleges and universities early in 1955. Eighty replies were received indicating whether the library carried on an educational program of its own and to what extent education about world affairs was included in the program. As reported in the *Journal of Higher Education*,[10] all but one of the reporting librarians indicated their support for the concept of the library as an educational agency responsible for initiating programs of its own, and all 80 of them reported some specific activities in education about world affairs in which their libraries engaged. There was a general desire expressed to do more in this field than they were doing. Among the handicaps reported were inadequacies of space, staff, and resources. Most inhibiting, however, in most places, was the persisting attitude of faculty and administration in regarding the library staff as service staff, not fully admitted to the educative function.

Table 1 indicates the activities bearing on education about world affairs which were carried on by 80 libraries, as indicated in the letters and reports received in answer to the inquiry.

TABLE 1

ACTIVITIES IN PROMOTION OF INTERNATIONAL UNDERSTANDING
CARRIED ON BY 80 LIBRARIES IN REPRESENTATIVE
COLLEGES AND UNIVERSITIES

Regular programs of exhibits	42
Bulletin board displays	39
Special exhibits	31
Technical assistance to groups interested in world affairs	25
Special rooms or collections of reading materials	21
Meeting space for interested student groups	15
Lists and reviews of books	10
Participation in radio and TV programing	9
Sponsorship of lectures and/or discussion groups	7
Personal activities of staff members	6
Use of foreign-student assistants	4
Sponsorship of concerts and art displays	3
Sponsorship of film programs	2
Encouragement of student personal libraries	2

[10] Howard E. Wilson and Gordon E. Samson, "The College Library in World Affairs," *Journal of Higher Education*, December 1955, pp. 479-86.

Exhibits are a part of the program of many libraries, and many of these exhibits deal with foreign cultures or with aspects of international relations. The exhibits are ordinarily teaching devices in themselves, as well as means for increasing reading by calling attention to books. A librarian queried in the Endowment survey reported a fairly typical situation:

The Library has 26 exhibition cases throughout the building which are changed on the average of once each month. Some exhibits are designed to impart information about a topic, others to encourage reading of a particular book or about a particular subject. Others are designed to publicize the library's holdings in some field or subject and some are designed to honor donors. At all times the Library has several cases devoted to world affairs. An estimated one-third of all exhibits are directly related to world affairs. They usually take two forms: "spot" exhibits featuring a particular country in which are arranged posters, pamphlets, and books about that country, or an exhibit giving information as well as showing material available about some current topic of political or economic significance which may or may not be a controversial topic.

Another librarian reports:

We have a fairly large number of foreign students on our campus and a staff member has been putting on from time to time a series of exhibits which include books, periodicals, handicrafts, pamphlets, and photographs of particular foreign countries. These exhibits have been arranged . . . in cooperation with students from these particular countries. . . . The results have been very satisfactory for students bring their own personal materials to use in the exhibits. Also, the exhibits are not under glass but are on bulletin board arrangements which make it possible for the brochures to be handled and looked at and the photographs to be examined closely. . . . Many of these exhibits commemorate some specific day in a particular country.

In one university a large entry hall of the library building serves as a central meeting place for students. On large bulletin boards, prominently placed, and on stands strategically distributed through the room, materials are effectively displayed. One display board always contains maps illustrating current world events. With a library staff effectively arranging a sequence of displays, and with large numbers of students using the attractive room, the displays are a highly educative influence. Too rarely, however, are library exhibits effectively synchronized with courses bearing on other nations or on international relations. Closer cooperation between library staff and specialists would give the display activities increased effectiveness.

Libraries often service student clubs with books and bibliographical aid, just as they do classes. Many librarians report serving International Relations Clubs and other student organizations such as are discussed in a later chapter of this report. About a third of the 80 libraries included in the survey have special collections or browsing rooms with special sections devoted to current events and world affairs. At the University of Denver and at the University of Southern California, for example, notable collections of books on world affairs are attractively housed and staffed in wings of the library building. Libraries frequently issue booklists of new acquisitions for the use of members of the college or university. One librarian writes:

I preface the monthly new booklist, which goes to our faculty and is available in various places to our students, with a single page of comment ranging over a wide area of library-connected subjects. Much of this comment I believe and hope has been of the kind that contributes to a broad view of the complexities of the world situation.

It is a custom on many campuses for the library to schedule lectures, some of which deal with world affairs. Most modern library buildings, such as that at the Massachusetts Institute of Technology, have music rooms where students hear recordings of the world's best music. Surprisingly enough, however, fairly few libraries in the survey of 80 institutions reported systematic development of book review sessions, such as are carried on effectively by public libraries like those in Cleveland and Baltimore.

The library on the campus is ordinarily an intellectual center, stimulating to students and faculty. Modern libraries express an educational concept which makes them a distinctive feature of academic life in the United States. For those who are concerned with making college life a positive influence in education about world affairs, the library, both in its services to classes and in its non-class, relatively informal activities, is a resource of power.

Campus Communication Agencies

Much that has been said about the educative potential in such campus focal points as the library, the chapel or religious center, and the college union, should also be said about other physical features of the college scene and the programs to which they may be dedicated. Galleries and museums lend themselves to exhibits, lectures, forums, which may throw light on cultural contacts and currents among nations. The theater, devoted either to student productions or to professional appearances, is no small conditioner of student thought about other nations and international contacts. The radio and television studios and programs which exist on many campuses are as influential on student thinking as their counterparts in the larger society are with adult citizens. At Indiana University, for example, according to the survey prepared in the Carnegie Endowment program:

> The Department of Radio presents programs concerned with Europe today. This series gives consideration to the peoples' home life, government, accomplishments, and culture. Countries which have been or will be treated are: France, Spain, Italy, Great Britain, Germany and Austria, Scandinavia, Poland and the Baltic nations, Russia, Yugoslavia, Czechoslovakia and Eastern Europe. A series which is being prepared will treat in some twenty short programs the Latin American countries. The Indiana University Round Table frequently discusses international problems. Folk music from foreign countries is often broadcast. The Department makes use of recorded materials from other countries: for example, Paris Star Time. At least one hour a day is given to the discussion of world problems in the news.[11]

[11] "The Indiana University in World Affairs Survey Report," *Universities and World Affairs*, Document No. 26 (Mimeographed; New York: Carnegie Endowment for International Peace, 1953), p. 9.

In the same way, films may be utilized to increase world understanding. Michigan State University reports the development of a Foreign Cinema Series which

. . . began with the showing of a few foreign-language films as a means of foreign-language instruction. It became so popular that it has become a regular feature of campus life. Fifteen to twenty films are shown each year. They comprise the best in French, German, Italian, Spanish, and Mexican films as well as a number of English films. . . . The admission charge is fifty cents. The films are patronized almost entirely by students and faculty. This series constitutes one of the most delightful as well as valuable features of the college program. Its effect is to create one of those intangible but significant currents that go to make for the "sophisticated mind." This series of cinema plays is an invaluable adjunct to all course programs in the field of international relations.[12]

Lectures and Assemblies

Inherent in the programs of college unions, chapels or religious centers, and libraries as educative agencies are lectures and large-group meetings. As will be indicated in a later chapter in an analysis of what students believe to be the sources of their ideas about world affairs, students rate lectures as more influential than many observers would assume. A group of 905 college seniors rated lectures as eighth in a group of 20 possible conditioners of their outlook; in an "intensity" rating, lectures dropped to twelfth place. When the same questionnaire was given, however, to 100 students who were particularly interested in world affairs, the average rating and the intensity rating of lectures rose markedly on the scale. Many students report themselves as stirred and influenced by the lecture occasion, by the speaker's personality, by the chance of "seeing an outstanding personage face to face"; the lecture occasion as well as the lecture content may be influential. Obviously lectures serve

[12] "Michigan State College and World Affairs," *Universities and World Affairs*, Document No. 69 (Mimeographed; New York: Carnegie Endowment for International Peace, 1954), p. 15.

many purposes: they may be interest-arousing; they may be informative for the already interested. While the great number of non-class lectures which students may attend probably flow over them like water over a dam, in the record of virtually all students are outstanding lectures which influenced markedly their orientation and thought.

Observation in many universities and colleges leads to the conclusion that, while lectures are widely scheduled and are reasonably well attended by college students and faculty, they are scheduled haphazardly and without much concern for their relation to the curriculum. In almost no institution is as much care given to an effective lecture program, capable of reaching and influencing large numbers of people, as is given to the preparation of a course which may touch only a few. There is evidence that large-group lectures, whether organized by the university administration or the union or the chapel or the library or other agency, are worth much more educative planning and creative thought than they ordinarily receive.

There is a value for the college in the general lecture quite apart from its substantive contribution to the total curriculum. That is the value of bringing large numbers of the campus citizens into face-to-face relationships with one another. In an earlier and simpler day, required chapel had the advantage of bringing all the members of the college together periodically, whatever complaints there may have been against compulsory attendance or sectarian instruction. Today on most campuses the fragmentation of social life has kept pace with the fragmentation of the curriculum; students come together in small groups for class instruction or for recreation, but infrequently do they experience the sight of the whole college or even any large segment of the college personnel, except perhaps at a football game, which may be one small reason why football as a spectator sport has become so popular in college life. Whether meetings for intellectual purposes are held in a chapel or in a field house, in the assembly room of a library or a union, or in a lecture hall, they help unify the college or the university. At the very least all-college meetings can put before students such symbols of the institution as the president—a functionary too commonly seen by large numbers of students only during freshmen orientation week and again when degrees are conferred.

At St. John's College in Annapolis, all-college lectures are held weekly, bringing to the campus carefully selected speakers competent to deal with specific questions of general interest, among them the conduct of world affairs. Attendance at the lectures is not compulsory but is traditional among St. John's students. As one recent graduate reports, "Had we missed a lecture, we'd have been lost in the campus bull sessions for the whole following week." It is obviously much easier to build up such a tradition of influential, non-course, all-college lectures in a smaller, somewhat rural institution having ready access to a source of good speakers. But too few universities have conscientiously tried to develop an urban and large-institution equivalent. At the University of California at Berkeley, President Sproul has for many years convened monthly "University Meetings." Held sometimes in the university's Greek Theater, and sometimes in the central crossroads plaza of the campus, they bring together relatively few of the students and faculty, yet bring them together more frequently and in larger numbers than on most other large campuses. And the most successful of the meetings have been those dealing with foreign affairs in which outstanding statesmen have been brought to the campus as speakers.

At Alabama College an experiment in long-range planning of all-college lectures has had both successes and failures. Some years ago the college undertook an ambitious plan for making weekly lectures a part of the general experience of students. Themes for the lecture series were carefully planned. The lectures were required of all students, but compulsory attendance provoked the usual student reactions. A plan for giving academic credit for the lectures, with marks based on a written examination covering their content, proved administratively unfeasible. The unpopularity of evening lectures caused a shift to a morning hour. Controversies over the topics dealt with led ultimately to a return to the more traditional convocation arrangements.

And yet the large meeting is certainly worth more administrative and faculty planning than it usually receives. In most colleges and universities it would be a significant contribution to student education, to faculty education, and to campus morale to provide a series of lectures, each notably done, with an examination at the end comparable to course examinations or to the general qualifying examinations required for graduation in some institutions. Under the impact of bigness we have developed the large lecture course, broken down weekly into small sectional meetings. It is equally feasible and desirable to develop the same plan in reverse, that of bringing together periodically for meetings on a topic of common interest a large number of smaller classes. In a program of area studies at Colgate each sophomore took a course dealing with one particular nation—Russia, France, Germany, for example. But periodically all sophomores came together to hear a lecture by an outside speaker on an important topic which cut across the lines of the various courses. Occasionally in many institutions an academic department schedules lectures for all students in the department. The suggestion made here is that campus unity, a sense of oneness in the college or university, can be cultivated, that a bridge can be built between classroom and assembly hall, and that vitalizing contributions can be made to education of students about world affairs by the convening of occasional large-group meetings which have curriculum status. Such meetings may offset the small-group fragmentation which so commonly afflicts colleges and universities.[13]

[13] See E. M. Hosman, "Convocations in Urban Universities," *School and Society*, March 5, 1938, pp. 316–18.

Even if the all-university assembly is impossible, we can at least move toward such larger-than-class meetings as are physically possible. The psychological effect on the campus may be ultimately good even though it takes time and the overcoming of resistance to build up support for such a program. Obviously, the mere bringing-together of all the members of the college for a brief time falls short of full participation or identification in community life, but there may be increased efficiency and heightened achievement in a less monotonous grouping of students than classes alone provide. And through such meetings, the resources of the campus may be more adequately used, and the program of education about world affairs may be enormously enriched. Such large-group meetings may be almost the only way to reach the great majority of college and university students with a presentation of materials on international matters. It would seem the part of wisdom to spend as much time and thought on developing a general lecture series on world affairs designed to reach all students as on developing an elementary course on international relations which, under the best of circumstances, attracts only a minute fraction of the total student body.

Housing Facilities and the International Outlook

The housing arrangements on most campuses have considerable possibility for awakening students to world points of view, particularly by providing the setting for friendships between American and foreign students. At the University of Florida, for example, all freshmen students are required to live in university dormitories. Testimony from upperclassmen indicates that the contact with foreign students in the freshman dormitories often cultivates enduring friendships and certainly alerts large numbers of students to the problems and potentialities of intercultural contacts. In 1953–54 the chief officer of the student government at Gainesville concerned with arousing interest in international relations among students was a student majoring in agriculture; he had not studied international relations in classes, but his whole student career had been influenced by friendships with foreign students made in the freshman dormitories. At a Midwest college, the plans for men's dormitories call for living quarters for units of eight men—four double bedrooms with a common living room—and it is planned to place one foreign student in each unit.

In every residential college visited by the author or conducting such a self-survey as the Carnegie Endowment has sponsored, the living arrangements in college dormitories and houses have been strikingly influential in shaping the relations between foreign and American students, and in conditioning the outlook on world affairs of many American students. Just as there is a demonstrable relationship between living arrangements and academic achievement, there is a relationship between living arrangements and cultural orientation of students.

The role of sororities and fraternities in facilitating friendships between American and foreign students, and in supporting the informal activities of campus life which influence the outlook of students cannot be ignored. As housing units for groups which provide a considerable proportion of student campus leaders, they not only offer opportunities for friendship among residents of a house but often determine the prestige and effectiveness of general campus activities bearing on world affairs. Williamson [14] has shown that, at the University of Minnesota, campus philanthropies, including funds for such international causes as are supported by World University Service, were markedly increased when fraternities and sororities as groups assumed responsibilities in campus campaigns and drives. At the same institution a student leader, influential in

[14] E. G. Williamson, B. J. Borreson, and Robert Irvine, "Learning Habits of Charitable Giving through the Extracurriculum," *Educational and Psychological Measurement*, Spring 1951, pp. 103–20.

many campus activities, reports that her thinking about other countries and our relations with them has been strikingly affected by having a foreign girl as a sorority roommate for two years.

On some campuses, sororities and fraternities hold aloof from foreign students; on others, student politicians, operating from tightly knit social groups, exploit selected foreign students for political purposes. But the attitude toward foreign students on the part of sororities and fraternities in American colleges and universities seems to be changing as rapidly as are the attitudes concerning discrimination based on color and race. Improvement in intergroup relations, domestic and international, on American campuses, with consonant reduction in prejudices, is a striking phenomenon of recent years.

Related to this liberalizing movement is the activity of very many sororities and fraternities in aiding foreign students, often by providing housing and meals. It is fairly common for social residence houses to be opened to foreign visitors for a period of time; on a good many campuses, student committees arrange for selected foreign students a sequence of house visits sufficient to provide room and board for a year. The Bowdoin Plan for receiving foreign students as guests of fraternities, developed by a veteran in 1947 as a memorial to a brother who had been killed in the war, is an early and widely copied example of such an arrangement. Under the Bowdoin Plan the college offers tuition scholarships to certain qualified students selected by undergraduate fraternities which, on their part, provide room and board for these men. At Stanford University a special student commission selects students, arranges with fraternities and sororities for their housing, and raises part of the additional funds needed. And in increasing number foreign students are admitted to full membership in fraternities and sororities. Considering the limited number of undergraduate foreign students on university campuses, and recognizing that graduate students are not ordinarily attracted to fraternity and sorority living, the rate of admission of foreign students to membership in the societies is encouraging.

One factor affecting education in world affairs which characterizes all living units, and particularly those with dining facilities, should be noted. Whether in a cooperative sorority at the University of Southern California, or in fraternity and sorority houses at Ohio State University, or in the residential houses at Harvard, or sponsored by a club dining in the college union, the friendly informal evening or dinner with invited guests who are competent and experienced in some phase of international relations is a vital influence on many students. A. Lawrence Lowell stressed the "dining and converation" provisions of the Harvard houses, saying they were "designed to make the intellectual life respectable at Cambridge." Students accord high rating as educative experience to such informal contacts with mature minds as these small-group, social situations provide. The substitution of capable, graduate-student, house leaders for house "mothers" in sororities and fraternities tends to encourage such "intellectual" activities. It should be added that institutions which have faculty housing appropriate for the reception of groups of students—as at Swarthmore, for example, where many of the honors seminars meet in the professors' homes—contribute effectively to the realistic education of students by the contacts such housing facilitates. At Mount Holyoke,

. . . in seven upper-class houses, a non-resident member of the faculty serves as house dean, and comes regularly two or three times weekly for dinner, tea, and other social functions. Associated with the house dean in each house are a group of honorary fellows—faculty, alumnae, trustees, and friends outside the College. These persons usually come on guest night and sometimes talk a few minutes after dinner to stimulate general conversation. It is the resident fellows who assume the major part of the responsibility in each house . . . in planning group activities and other aspects of living together. These resident fellows may spend one-third of their time on graduate study. They work on college projects, students' interests, and house libraries.

Most of these features of the Holyoke plan result in closer relationship between the academic and the non-academic phases of college life.[15]

The Campus of the Future

It would be possible to continue indefinitely a cataloguing of the non-class, nonformal resources on the typical American campus for education about world affairs. Indeed, there are on many campuses successful uses of these resources. These "promising practices" must be recognized before it is also emphasized that on no campus are all the available resources used, and on most campuses very few of them are focused or coordinated in any systematic fashion.

Obviously, educational activities made possible through these nonformal assets of university life are not easily organized and coordinated. When controlled or preplanned in any mechanical fashion they lose their effectiveness. They depend upon the alertness and sensitivity of members of the college, particularly of older members. They can be stimulated and can be more nearly orchestrated than is customary only if faculty as well as administrators and students feel a sense of responsibility for them. There is no pattern of activities nor prescription for their effective coordination which can be universally applied. The physical structure of each college plant, more enduring even than the traditions of the college, condition what can be done and how it can be molded into a meaningful and educative collegiate way of life.

The informal approach through libraries, assemblies, college unions, international houses, nationality houses and rooms, living arrangements, and religious centers is, however, of particular importance in collegiate education about world affairs. In a society such as ours, where public opinion is active and leadership of public opinion is crucial, it seems obvious that all college

[15] Ruth Strang, *Group Activities in College and Secondary School* (Rev. ed.; New York: Harper & Bros., 1946), p. 280.

graduates need to be concerned and reasonably informed about foreign policies, about world cultures, about international relations. That is almost a prerequisite for the successful, democratic conduct of international relations. In the typical institution of higher education a relatively small proportion of the graduates have been exposed to any systematic instruction about international relations. It is the rare program even in general education which provides direct teaching about the international facts of life. This situation in formal instruction is not likely to be altered radically in the immediate future. This fact makes it extremely important for the individuals and organizations which seek better understanding and orientation on world affairs for all college students to utilize fully every possible resource of a nonformal character and to relate these nonformal developments to class offerings as supplementary and coordinate.

Having examined the "facilities for learning" in addition to the classrooms and laboratories which compose the college habitat, and pondered on the manner and extent to which these facilities can contribute to effective education about world affairs, one begins to formulate a conception of an "ideal campus" in terms of such education. On such a campus, in addition to the best program of courses which can be designed, there will be available for all students carefully planned experiences calculated to sensitize them to the basic issues of international relations, acquaint them with the concepts of cultural differentiation and interpenetration, widen geographic horizons, stimulate interests in world affairs, afford training in thoughtful solution of international questions, and equip students with pertinent information and concepts. From that ideal campus would go graduates who, in their various professions and communities, would have the will and the knowledge to become leaders in the public determination of policy respecting international matters.

The campus of this ideal institution, whether urban or rural, large or small, public or private, would contain items of beauty, designed to stir the emotions of the members of the college, and among these items would be visible products of the cultures of other lands. The ideal university will have found alumni in all parts of the world to provide these tangible evidences of the wide brotherhood bound together in alma mater.

Among the facilities will be a college union in which members of the college meet in recreation, in friendship, in study, at conferences and lectures and forums and exhibits, each, within reason, contributing to international contacts and deeper and more sensitive understanding of world realities. Across the way will be another center of student life, the library, with its browsing rooms, exhibits of new books on world cultures and contacts, its music room where music from all the world is heard, its oral book reviews, its map room to contribute to the students' sense of space and location and distance, and its other aids to study, both formal and informal. And a chapel or assembly hall will provide space for bringing large numbers of the members of the college into face-to-face contact with great speakers whose experiences and insights contribute to the education of young men and women.

In the out-of-class activities of students, those activities by which they strenuously prepare for the community life of America, will be constant reminders and insights into world affairs. There will be provision for intermingling socially and intellectually with students from all parts of the world. There will be a cultivation of personal responsibility for participation in civic decisions on international policies. There will be preparation of leaders for community enterprises, for vocational and professional fields, who are alert and sensitive to the international factors which condition the national welfare and security.

——————————————CHAPTER THREE

Members of the College

The college in the Greek sense is a group of men face to face with one another; and a community of minds is not the narrow reference of one specialist to another or specialized function of mind to another but an association of men in all their diversity and wholeness.—Baker Brownell, The College and the Community

The most potent educational influence of Oxford and Cambridge has been found outside lecture room or laboratory and even outside the private hour with the tutor. It arises, indirectly, from the character of the community life. No passage in Newman is better remembered or more frequently quoted than that in which he depicts and extols the influence of students on one another and asserts that if he had to choose between one system in which students lived a corporate life but received no formal teaching and were submitted to no examination and another in which they were rigorously examined but lived no corporate life, he would unhesitatingly prefer the former.—Sir Walter Moberley, The Crisis in the University

THE MEMBERS of a college or university are themselves resources for education about world affairs, exerting a mutual influence on one another in all the contacts of college life. The members of the college include administrators, faculty, and students. Among them are individuals and groups with unusual background and insight on other cultures and on the conduct of foreign policy and international relations. Testimony of stu-

71

dents and alumni indicates that these human resources within the college community are a major determinant of what students think and feel and understand. The influence of contact is exerted in classrooms and clubs, in college journalism, in social affairs, in the union, in assemblies, in bull sessions, and in the total community life of the institution.

This chapter examines the present generation of faculty and students on American campuses with particular reference to the factors or characteristics of the college population which influence collegiate education about world cultures and international relations. While the two main divisions of college members, faculty and students, are examined in separate sections of the chapter, the separation is only for purposes of convenient analysis. The chapter as a whole is built upon the concept developed in chapter 1, that there is increasing integration of classroom and out-of-class experience, and that the total range of contacts between students and faculty is a part of college education. The chapter as a whole stresses the common interests and mutual relations among all members of the college.

The Faculty

To describe, let alone analyze, faculty members as a group in American society is by no means a simple task. Descriptive statistics, even of the most generalized sort, are inadequate. Few comprehensive sociological analyses, such as Logan Wilson made in 1942 in *The Academic Man*,[1] are available. A few documentary novels treat of professors or faculty mores in psychological terms. The data on which to base a picture of the faculty as citizens of the college are grossly inadequate. The data indicative of faculty concerns and insights into world cultures and international contacts are scattered and incomplete.

[1] Wilson, *The Academic Man* (New York: Oxford University Press, 1942).

The United States Office of Education reports that in 1951–52 a total of 244,488 persons were employed on the administrative and instructional staffs of institutions of higher education in the United States.[2] This number covered colleges, universities, professional schools, teachers colleges, and junior colleges, and included a considerable number of part-time professors. The same report estimated the full-time equivalent of the group to be approximately 198,000. Dael Wolfle estimated in 1953 that there were some 200,000 full-time faculty—19 percent in the natural sciences, 13 percent in the social sciences including psychology, 25 percent in humanities and arts, 11 percent in education, and the remainder in scattered professional fields.[3]

In 1954 the Research Division of the National Education Association reported a comprehensive survey dealing with "Instructional Staff Practices and Policies in Degree-Granting Institutions."[4] Eliminating junior colleges and special schools, the Research Division addressed an inquiry to the 1,002 degree-granting institutions listed in the *Education Directory: 1953–54* of the Office of Education, including public and private, large and small institutions. Six hundred and seventy-nine institutions, or 67.8 percent of the total, replied, indicating that they employed a total of 70,646 instructional staff members. Of these, 26.8 percent were professors, 21.8 percent associate professors, 30.4 percent assistant professors, and 21 percent instructors. About 3 percent of the instructors and 84 percent of the pro-

---

[2] U. S. Office of Education, Department of Health, Education, and Welfare, "Statistics of Higher Education: Faculty, Students, and Degrees, 1951–52," *Biennial Survey of Education in the United States, 1950–52* (Washington: Government Printing Office, 1955), sec. I, chap. 4.

[3] Unpublished manuscript of J. F. Wellemeyer, Jr., American Council of Learned Societies, 1953, as quoted in Dael Wolfle, *America's Resources of Specialized Talent: A Current Appraisal and a Look Ahead* (New York: Harper & Bros., 1954), pp. 124–25.

[4] Research Division, National Education Association, "Instructional Staff Practices and Policies in Degree-Granting Institutions, 1953–54," *Research Bulletin*, December 1954, pp. 159–214.

fessors had doctor's degrees, and the great majority of the total possessed at least the master's degree.

Within the faculty there are several groups, overlapping in membership, which have special capacity for influencing the world outlook of students. Among these groups may be listed (1) specialists in the study of international relations, (2) specialists in the study of cultures other than our own, (3) those who have studied and lived abroad and who maintain international contacts in their academic specializations, and (4) the group, drawn from many academic fields and increasing in number, which has had experience in the actual conduct of some aspect of international affairs or of foreign policy. Certain observations about each of these four groups and about their influence on the college community as a whole may be made, but the observations are general and become significant only as they are tested in the individual circumstances of each college or university. Each of these groups is a major resource for an institution; each should be utilized consciously and in ways appropriate to its character within each institution. Ordinarily, colleges and universities are making systematic use of specialists in the study of international relations and of world areas, but are not consciously or systematically using to the full the backgrounds of travel and experience abroad which are possessed by many faculty members.

Within the last half-century specialists in international relations have made their appearance on the faculties of most institutions of higher education in America. During that period the subject or discipline of international relations has developed and has taken form in course offerings and university programs. Other volumes in the Carnegie Endowment series deal with the subject of international relations in the undergraduate curriculum and with the training of specialists in this field, but it may be pointed out here that in recent years the subject of international relations has widened beyond the study of international law and beyond the field of political science. Approaches to analysis of foreign policy and international relations through psychology, demography, modern languages, natural resources, anthropology, and particularly economics and trade are to be found in many college catalogues. However, even through all the classes embodying these varied approaches the specialists in international relations reach only a limited proportion of students. Courses in the stricter concept of international relations as concerned with international organization and politics are taken by relatively few students. Classroom contacts between specialists in international relations, thus defined, and student bodies are not numerically extensive even though they may be qualitatively extremely good.

Instructors in world affairs, however, have a status of influence on students out of proportion to their numbers on the faculty. Their influence is more nearly attuned to the relation of their discipline to interest-challenging public events than to its recency of arrival in academic fields or to formal enrollment in the classes they teach. Their influence is exerted within the academic community by more than proportionate attention to their field in public lectures, forums, institutes, radio, and press. These specialists have knowledge which is frequently of high concern to members of the college because of its relation to current events. Their expertness is in continual demand beyond the classroom; they frequently have out-of-class prestige among students as commentators on issues which concern all citizens. Students who do not take courses in international relations testify, as will be shown later, to the importance of informal contact with specialists in the field.

Much the same can be said for specialists in the study of world areas. World-area centers exist in many institutions, which have an informal campus influence directly proportionate to the position of the area in current news. To the degree that language instruction has become an avenue into the culture of an area, the linguistic interpreters of the culture are also sought out by students looking for the background to the news.

It would be a serious mistake, however, to limit an inventory of faculty resources in education about world matters to the specialists in international relations or in area studies. A large proportion of the total faculty group in most American institutions has had educative experience in countries outside the United States, and their background has pervasive influence in the contacts of college life.

Many faculty members are deeply involved in the international relations of their own disciplines. The survey reports from colleges and universities which cooperated during the years 1950–55 in the Carnegie Endowment's program on universities and world affairs provide evidence of the degree to which faculty members have had worth-while experience abroad, giving them insight at least potentially influential in the college community. In virtually every institutional self-survey some form of tabulation of faculty experience, background, training, and interest was made. In a group of 17 institutions the polling procedures were sufficiently similar to warrant combining them in a generalized picture. In the 17 colleges and universities were 4,707 faculty members; 2,478 of these provided data about themselves. Of this number 1,291 had traveled abroad; of these 649 had studied or worked abroad for a considerable period of time; 112 of the group held degrees from academic institutions outside the United States. A very large proportion of the group knew at least one foreign language, and many of them several languages. A large number of American professors maintain contact with scholars abroad, write books and articles which circulate beyond the country, keep themselves informed of researches conducted by their "opposite numbers" abroad, occasionally attend international conferences and institutes and seminars.

Certain specific institutions may illustrate the wealth of this faculty resource. Pennsylvania State University had in 1951 a faculty of 2,100 people. About a third of these—778—replied to a questionnaire[5] revealing that 447 had traveled abroad, over half of them working or studying abroad for a period of more than six months. Fifty faculty members had taught abroad; 14 had been born and educated abroad. At Wellesley College, with a faculty of 178, a questionnaire was filled out by 125, indicating that 102 had been abroad, 37 had studied in other countries, and 21 had received degrees from foreign institutions.[6] At Texas Christian University 78 percent of a faculty of 167 had traveled outside the United States.[7]

In the self-survey made by a faculty committee at the State University of Iowa in 1953–55, a questionnaire "designed to reveal the nature and extent of their foreign experiences and international contacts" was sent to the 782 professors and instructors on the staff. Four hundred and fifty-four (58 percent) of the questionnaires were filled out and returned. The report which analyzes these data draws the following conclusions:

Fifty-six of the 454 (12.3 percent) were born in a foreign country. . . . Of the 56 born abroad, 17 received all or nearly all of their schooling in the United States. Four completed elementary school; 7 completed high school, and 21 took most or all of their college work in their native lands. . . .

Of the (398) American-born faculty members responding, 37 (9.3 percent) had secured some formal education abroad; 5 had obtained a doctor's degree in a foreign country. Twenty-eight had studied in Europe, 4 in Mexico, 2 in Canada, and 1 each in Australia, New Zealand, and China.

Of the 454 respondents, 115 (25 percent) had engaged since 1946 in what they regarded as significant travel, spending on the average 5.6 months in one or more foreign countries. . . . The purposes of

[5] "A World-Affairs Survey of the Pennsylvania State University," *Universities and World Affairs*, Document No. 39 (Mimeographed; New York: Carnegie Endowment for International Peace, 1954), p. 9.

[6] "Wellesley Report," *Universities and World Affairs*, Document No. 8 (Mimeographed; New York: Carnegie Endowment for International Peace, 1952), pp. 25–28.

[7] "Texas Christian University in International Affairs," *Universities and World Affairs*, Document No. 34 (Mimeographed; New York: Carnegie Endowment for International Peace, 1954), pp. 17–20.

travel were generally of a professional nature: study and research, lecturing and teaching, and attending professional meetings.

Thirty-nine (8.6 percent) indicated that they had served as experts with international organizations or other governments. . . . Thirty-three (7.2 percent) had been employed by United States government agencies concerned with foreign relations. . . . Eleven had held lectureships or Fulbright appointments abroad. Five others had engaged in special activities such as scientific expeditions or news reporting.

One hundred and seventy (37 percent) reported that they maintained personal contacts with scholars and friends abroad.[8]

The staff members with foreign experience and contacts came from all departments of the university. The survey committee felt that this background of experience influenced campus life considerably, not merely by affecting class instruction and curriculum content, but by a quickening of general campus interest and alertness in foreign matters.

Exchange of Scholars

Programs for interchange of persons, both governmental and nongovernmental, which have developed particularly since 1945, are now beginning to influence substantially the experience and outlook of faculties in American universities. Comprehensive data for the academic year 1953–54 were obtained by the Institute of International Education in a nation-wide survey dealing with American faculty members abroad on "teaching or educational assignments."[9] Eighty percent (1,483 of the 1,851 institutions polled) replied to a questionnaire, reporting that 1,047 United States professors, instructors, and lecturers were abroad in that one year on teaching assignments, or government missions, or for special research tasks. Of these, 588 (56.2

[8] "The State University of Iowa and World Affairs," *Universities and World Affairs,* Document No. 80 (Mimeographed; New York: Carnegie Endowment for International Peace, 1955), pp. 4–5.

[9] "Survey of United States Professors, Instructors, and Lecturers Abroad, 1953–54" (Mimeographed; New York: Institute of International Education, 1955).

percent) were in Europe, 190 (18.1 percent) in Far Eastern countries, and 101 (9.6 percent) in the Near and Middle East. The United Kingdom attracted 129, France 82, Germany 79, Italy 52, while another 108 traveled in more than one European country; 42 were in India, 36 in Japan, 34 in the Philippines, 24 in Iran, and 20 in Pakistan.

Almost 70 percent of the total 1,047 pursued work in ten academic fields—138 in languages, 98 in agriculture, 78 in history, 73 in education, 69 in sociology, 68 in creative arts, 60 in literature, 48 in economics, 47 in political science, and 46 in the biological sciences. They came from all parts of the United States, though ten states accounted for three-fifths of the total, with New York and California sending substantially more than other states. More than half who reported financial data indicated they went abroad assisted by government grant, while foundations accounted for a fifth of the total. No adequate studies have yet been made of the influence on campus of men and women who have returned from serious work abroad; yet every informal report indicates the very great significance of their experience on the cosmopolitanism of college life. Moreover, under present circumstances, their influence will be felt in cumulative degree.

This is not the place to analyze existing governmental and foundation programs for exchange of professors and research workers; that has been done in many other places. It should be pointed out, however, that a fairly extensive informal survey of American colleges and universities fails to locate many institutions that have a planned program for making faculty exchanges contribute fully to the long-range development of the institution or to the collegiate life of the campus. The administration and faculty of George Peabody College for Teachers have launched a program designed ultimately to provide (through systematic utilization of government and foundation opportunities) foreign experience for every faculty member of professorial rank. But few college administrations have an over-all, long-range plan for enriching the institutional life or for building up particular departments through arrangement for faculty travel; too few take the initiative in securing travel aid for faculty where it can be of greatest service to both the person and the institution. The initiative and responsibility for securing travel grants ordinarily lies with the person; many able people for whom travel would be excellent development do not find the opportunity. In institutional as well as individual planning for faculty travel and exchange lies a significant avenue of academic development.

A considerable number of visiting faculty members from outside the United States are residents in American institutions each year, and these visitors are often outstanding members of the academic community, influential in curricular and extra-curricular affairs. The Institute of International Education conducted a survey which illustrates this situation as of 1954–55.[10] Questionnaires were mailed to 1,851 institutions of higher education listed in the *Education Directory: 1953–54*, asking for the name, sex, sponsoring agencies, field of interest, and country of citizenship of foreign faculty members. Refugee scholars and applicants for United States citizenship were excluded from the survey.

Replies were received from 79.7 percent of the colleges and universities, indicating that in 1954–55 there were 635 foreign professors, instructors, lecturers, and assistants at work in these American institutions. Of the 635, a total of 336 came from Europe, 129 from Far Eastern countries, and 110 from Canada and Central America. The United Kingdom provided 127 of the visitors. These, with 54 from Nationalist China, 48 from Canada, 39 from India, 38 from Germany, 37 from France, 27 from Japan, 20 from Switzerland, and 18 each from Italy and

[10] *Open Doors: A Report on Three Surveys—Foreign Students, Foreign Faculty Members, Foreign Doctors—in the United States, 1954–1955* (New York: Institute of International Education, 1955), pp. 11–13, 50–51.

the Netherlands, accounted for two-thirds of the total. More of the visitors were in the natural sciences than in any other field (197), with 149 in the humanities, 137 in medicine, and 71 in the social sciences. While the total group was quite widely distributed, ten states received almost 72 percent of them— New York with 103, Pennsylvania with 80, Minnesota with 66, followed in order by Massachusetts, Wisconsin, Indiana, California, Texas, New Jersey, and Ohio.

The influence of this group of visiting faculty members from outside the United States can, of course, only be speculated on. Some of the visitors do not come in contact with large groups of students; others become campus personalities affecting substantially the climate of opinion within the campus communities. While college life baffles many of the visitors and irritates some, a majority seem to appreciate the informality of student-professor relations and often to be enthusiastic over the total educative effect of the American college environment.

Professors with Public Experience

Of perhaps greatest educational influence on the academic community is the considerable number of faculty members in most universities and colleges who in recent years have been directly involved in some phase of the work of international agencies or in the formation or operation of American foreign policy, including military occupation and technical assistance. Not only are there many veterans of military campaigns and occupation governments now on the faculties, but substantial numbers have been involved in technical assistance to underdeveloped areas, in such activities as are sponsored by the World Health Organization and UNESCO, in the United States Information Agency, in diplomatic and cultural missions, and in private business abroad. Sixty-seven out of 454 faculty members at the State University of Iowa, in the survey reported earlier in this chapter, indicated that they had been employed for a period by governmental or intergovernmental agencies.

Contact with these faculty members who have demonstrated their competence in the actual operation of some phase of foreign policy as well as in their classroom instruction is regarded by students who have had such contact as highly influential on their undergraduate thinking about world affairs. There is a sense in which many of these specialists in widely varied disciplines who have demonstrated their own mastery of a field and the direct importance of that field to world affairs are now the professors with prestige, the personalities in the academic community. They have become leaders in the academic community through general activities on the campus as well as in their classrooms. When a professor of agriculture at Minnesota, who has directly influenced the wheat crops of countries all over the world, gives a campus lecture, students go to hear him as students went, in an earlier day, to hear Copeland at Harvard or Phelps at Yale. A professor of law at Columbia who negotiated the ending of the Berlin blockade, a scientist at Chicago who helped harness atomic energy, and their counterparts on faculties all across the country, are significantly influential in establishing the mind sets and the attitudes and the accepted values of the college community. Their words are listened to at the faculty clubs and in public forums; they are quoted in the campus press, and their opinions reverberate in the endless bull sessions of students.

Even this brief examination of the faculty characteristics which constitute special resources for education about world affairs is suggestive of relatively new influences in American college life. In all probability, professors more than any other occupational group in American society have knowledge of foreign cultures and have experience abroad, either in the conduct of aspects of international relations or in studies arising in their fields of specialization. Moreover, the campus environment provides unusual opportunities for drawing upon the insight and experience thus gained not only through formal class work but also through the endless conversations, meetings, club activities, and cocurricular programs of college life.

Unfortunately, while the foreign experience of a faculty member is often reflected in the courses he offers, on many campuses provision is not made for use of this resource in non-class activities except as a matter of chance. There seems to be little systematic follow-up of Fulbright returnees, for example, in order to assure that the whole college benefits by their experience abroad. Relatively few colleges have an adequate inventory of the foreign interests, contacts, insights, or hobbies of their faculties. Foreign travel, leadership in professional organizations, and government service do not count largely in determining promotion, as revealed by the study of the Research Division of the National Education Association already cited. In the same study community service and relationship with students are placed last on the list of factors determining promotion. Under such circumstances, there is relatively little administrative stimulus for the full, coordinated, and informal utilization of the resources of interest and knowledge possessed by the traveled men and women who are among the institution's senior citizens. Too many faculty members have more to give to the education of students about world cultures and affairs than the circumstances of college living enable or prod them to give.

American Students

The student body of American institutions of higher education has no counterpart in all history, both as to size in relation to the total population and as to wide-ranging interests, motives, and career objectives. In the European tradition, university students are almost by definition preprofessional students, but in American colleges and universities of today are to be found not only pre-medical, pre-legal, and pre-theological students, but also—often in very large numbers and in close juxtaposition— pre-business, pre-agriculture, pre-labor, pre-teaching, pre-secretarial, pre-managerial, pre-salesman, pre-public relations, pre-homemaking, and pre-men-about-town students. The considerable number of young Americans who are aimlessly in college, without specific focus to their interests, is in marked contrast to students elsewhere. No student body has ever been so representative of the total population or of the total occupational range of a nation as is the American student body of the 1950's. The student members of American college and university communities are not a separate class or caste; their ties with the mass influences of American life are close and strong. They neither have nor commonly ask for a separate niche in the structure and culture of the national society. To be a college man or woman in Canby's day was to be in an elite group, but to be in college today is, relatively speaking, only a matter of course, almost an expected situation for reasonably able American youth.

The proportion of the total American population of college age which is enrolled in institutions of higher education is extremely high. As has been pointed out, "One of the noteworthy things about higher education in the United States is that there is so much of it." Between 1870 and 1940, while the population of the country was increasing threefold, the college population was increasing thirtyfold. Today approximately one-fifth of all American youth go to college. This is roughly five times the proportion in England, six or seven times that in Germany, and ten times that of France.

The 2,296,592 students in American institutions in 1950 represented a growth from 237,592 in 1900, a tenfold increase in fifty years. As the veterans completed their college programs, enrollments temporarily declined in the early 1950's but by 1955 an upward swing heralded almost an avalanche of students.

In that year enrollments reached the figure of 2,477,847, with predictions of 2,900,000 college students in 1960, and 4,500,000 in 1970. Obviously, this rise in enrollments presents the American people and their institutions of higher education with enormous and complex problems; it may be that coming years will witness drastic alterations in the nature and structure of American higher education. The task of the present chapter, however, is not that of dealing with those problems and portents. Rather, the point here made is that the members of American colleges today are, and in all probability will be for the proximate future, an extraordinarily representative cross section of the total American population and of the American cultural characteristics. This fact bears pertinently on our inquiry, for the same factors which make the American people increasingly concerned with foreign relations and world affairs increase the interests and sensitivities and worries of college students in this field. The analyses of student interests referred to later in this chapter amply indicate this fact, and many of the campus activities to be described rest upon the foundation of these interests, shared by the whole citizenry of the United States during this era.

The general picture of America's college population is obviously but background for analysis of the student members of any specific college community. There are, of course, men's institutions and women's institutions, but the vast majority of American colleges and universities are coeducational. They vary extremely in size, with the largest student group, of over 40,000, at New York University. The ten largest institutions in the fall of 1954 enrolled a total of 260,264 students, but the United States Office of Education listed in that year 955 colleges with fewer than 500 students each. One of the chief distinguishing characteristics of American higher education is the extreme diversity of its institutions. Each college has its tradition, sometimes artificially cultivated, but powerful in its attraction to particular students and highly influential in determining the quality of the campus. To know the students without knowing also their particular collegiate locale is to see the college population inadequately. While the standardizing influences of American life and the mobility of students and faculty and college administrators tend to emphasize similarities among institutions of higher education, those who would appraise a particular institution must become familiar with its distinctive features. No generalized description of students can do justice to the distinctive qualities of each campus population.

At the risk of unwarranted generalization, however, it may be possible to suggest certain broad characteristics of college students of the 1950's which have direct bearing on education about world affairs. Students in this decade, as was indicated in chapter 1 and will be amplified in later chapters, have a new status in our colleges and universities. They have assumed a more responsible partnership in the management of higher education, have a voice in both curricular and extracurricular affairs, and are more effectively organized than ever before. The character and quality of the student body is of consequence to the development of higher education itself by virtue of the new role that students now play.

First it must be noted that students now tend to be chronologically older than in earlier college generations. Colonial college students were of what we call high school age. Even after the American academic ladder was established and admission to higher education rested on a foundation of twelve years of schooling, students in college were ordinarily in the age bracket seventeen to twenty-two. Two factors have tended to raise this age. As it became more customary for young men and women to work their way through college, often with delay in the pursuit of their academic degrees, the average age of students was lifted. Of much more importance, the arrival on campus of veterans, whether of World War II or of Korea or simply of military training, has made the college population older. This increasing age appears more clearly in the universities than in the colleges, partly because the larger institutions are more likely to attract older students and partly because the dividing line between graduate and undergraduate courses is often blurred. On the whole this relative maturity of students is excellent both for the individual and for the institution. An editor of the *Atlantic Monthly* is said to have remarked on one occasion, "Boys are sent to Harvard to grow up. Would that I had grown up and then been sent to Harvard." His wish for himself and his institution is now turning into reality for great numbers of young Americans in many institutions, largely because of economic and military considerations. Some deans still say that students like to be treated like men and women while things are going well but like boys and girls when crises come. Many observers point out how much younger American college students are than are university students in Europe. But even so, the average age of American students, and with it their level of maturity, is rising.

Students are relatively mature today in more than a chronological sense. In Canby's day at Yale college was likely to be a sheltered prelude to the reality of adult existence, for both the grinds and the playboys. The tendency in American culture to prolong childhood has been frequently noted by anthropologists; it has been traditional to protect young people, to shelter them from out-of-school and out-of-college realities. American college students, for example, in contrast to students elsewhere have traditionally had no place in American political life. The residential college earlier prided itself on being a miniature society rather than a segment of the whole society. In recent years, however, the situation has tended to change. The curriculum itself has reflected closer interest in the outside world, as in Dartmouth's course on Great Issues or in many of the introductory orientation courses in the social sciences and the humanities, and as in the increased occupational concerns of such colleges as those of business administration or agriculture.

With much more than half the total student population earning at least part of their way through college as well as with the utilitarian motivations of many college programs, the economic "facts of life" are now relatively well known to many undergraduates. And of even more universal import is the influence of military service in an era of insecurity. Both the veterans of military service and those who are faced with service are uneasily alert to the current international situation as it affects the demand for military manpower. More students are today more intimately and actively concerned with the realities of public affairs, particularly affairs affecting national security, than were students in the 1920's. In a real sense, the college age group which is drawn on for military service and which is in some states already empowered to vote, is mature because it has a front-row place in the nation's manpower reservoir. Students today are less secure and less isolated, more alert to outside events and more sensitive to public as well as private problems.

The geographic horizons of students today are much wider than formerly, in spite of the fact that the formal study of geography is still neglected in American higher education. The present generation of students has been made familiar with far places by radio and newspapers and films, and, in some cases, by personal travel in military service or, as will be shown later, in summer study tours. A relatively cosmopolitan group appears on almost every campus. While it is still true that easy geographic accessibility to college is an important factor in motivating students to enroll in college, the mobility of American college students is very great. A number of institutions stand out as national centers, with recruitment and selection programs blanketing the country. But also a small college in Illinois attracted in 1954 students from four times as many states as it did a quarter of a century earlier when the college itself was better known. There are very few campus communities which attract a purely local group except among the junior colleges or specifically community colleges, and even these are rarely insulated from wider interests and contacts.

Maturity does not necessarily mean that students are less motivated by utilitarian or practical concerns in respect to their education. There seems to be no widespread turning to study of the meaning of life, of philosophy, of the humanities. Even the current revival of interest in religion seems not deeply rooted on most of the country's campuses.[11] Without undue selfishness on the student's part there is a considerable tendency to calculate the future effect of present actions, and in some students, though by no means all, an inclination to play it safe, to avoid sticking one's neck out unnecessarily. At the same time there is no lack of altruism, of concern over freedom, of willingness to work for worthy causes. In fact, the crusading humanitarian zeal which, half a century ago, was much more characteristic of women's colleges than of colleges in general, is now a pervasive influence. Students raise substantial amounts of money or material for such agencies as the World University Service and other philanthropic causes. They are quick to sympathy and readily stirred to action when perceiving there is something they can do for human welfare. Their support of UNESCO, for example, has been primarily in terms of programs of relief and rehabilitation in which personal humanitarian action rather than theoretical consideration was involved.

There are many factors, then, in the character of the student body which tend to rouse students' interest in world affairs. A survey of 500 students at the University of Florida in 1954

[11] For discussion of religion among college students see, John Sloan Dickey, "Conscience and the Undergraduate," *Atlantic Monthly*, April 1955, pp. 31–35.

indicates the extent of the interest.[12] When asked about the degree of interest they had in world affairs 13 percent of the 500 students said "very much," 32 percent indicated ordinary interest, 35 percent said they "could take it or leave it," 20 percent found the subject boring. Interest among upperclassmen was substantially greater than for freshmen and sophomores. Significantly, upperclassmen rated the situation in Asia as responsible for their increased interest. In a survey made in connection with the Carnegie Endowment program 891 seniors in 50 institutions in 1954 indicated their interest in world affairs. Of the 891 a group of 531 professed "very much" interest in international matters, 323 indicated ordinary interest, 31 could "take it or leave it," and six rated the subject as something to avoid. Of 844 students in the group, 253 women and 291 men (a total of 544) reported that they habitually read magazine articles and newspaper items dealing with international matters. There is little doubt that most students feel a personal involvement in international matters, and that the conditions and activities of campus life as well as of the classroom reflect that interest.

Foreign Students

Not only does life in college facilitate contacts with persons from different sections of the United States and from the varied social and ethnic and political groups in the country, but it also now affords most American students opportunity for association with other nationals. Prior to World War II it was possible for most American students to go through four years of college without ever seeing a student from another land. Today, with more than 34,000 foreign students widely distributed among

[12] The survey was made in connection with the Carnegie Endowment program by Bill Dugger, Jr., and Charles Hoffman, students, working under the direction of Dr. Ivan Putman. Mr. Dugger, as Secretary for International Affairs in the Cabinet of the President of the Student Council, was primarily responsible for the survey.

American colleges and universities, it is almost impossible for an American student to avoid meeting and knowing a student embodiment of another culture. In our student population there is one foreign student for every 70 American students.

The presence of large numbers of foreign students in the United States is an educative influence of considerable power. Another volume in this series, *Foreign Students and Higher Education in the United States,* deals with the problems and adjustments of foreign students. It reports a growing volume of research about the foreign members of American colleges. While research on the effect of an American sojourn on foreign students is under way, there has been relatively little analysis of the effect of foreign students on the American student body. Yet American students, in questionnaire and in direct response to conversational inquiries, attest consistently that the opportunity of meeting substantial numbers of students from widely scattered countries and cultures is an important educative factor in the experience of being in college.

According to a census taken by the Institute of International Education, 34,232 foreign students were registered in a total of 1,629 American institutions during the academic year 1954–55.[13] These students come from "129 different nations, dependent areas, trust territories, and international and military areas." Of these 34,232 students, 30 percent come from the Far East, 25 percent from Latin America, 15 percent from Europe, 13 percent from Canada, 13 percent from the Near and Middle East, and the remainder from Africa and Oceania. Eight countries sent more than a thousand students each to the United States for the year 1954–55: Canada, 4,362; Nationalist China, 3,637; India, 1,679; Japan, 1,572; the Philippine Republic, 1,476; Colombia, 1,301; Mexico, 1,247; and Korea, 1,197. There were 710 students from the United Kingdom, 472 from France, 881 from Greece, 759 from Germany, and a total of 770 from the

[13] See *Open Doors,* op. cit., pp. 6–10, 17–32, 39–43.

Scandinavian countries. Of particular interest in these figures is the great number from Asia, distant culturally even more than geographically from the United States. More than half of the total number of foreign students were undergraduates, with Canada and Latin America leading in this category. Half of the foreign students were under twenty-five years in age, and nearly 6,000 of them were over thirty. Slightly more than a quarter of the foreign students were women.

According to the Institute survey:

Foreign students are studying in every state, the District of Columbia, Alaska, the Canal Zone, Hawaii, and Puerto Rico. Nearly two-thirds of the foreign student population, however, is concentrated in New York, California, Massachusetts, Michigan, Illinois, Pennsylvania, Texas, Indiana, Ohio, and the District of Columbia.

Two institutions have more than 1,000 foreign students enrolled. . . . Columbia University (1,254), the University of California (1,238). New York University, the University of Michigan, Harvard University, Massachusetts Institute of Technology, the University of Illinois, the University of Southern California, and the University of Minnesota have between 500 and 1,000 foreign students.[14]

At Massachusetts Institute of Technology one out of every ten students is a foreign visitor; among the ten universities enrolling the greatest number of foreign students, not less than one out of twenty-five registrants is from outside the United States. In a group of twenty widely distributed liberal arts colleges, not attached to universities, foreign students compose from 1 to 7 percent of the student body.

As has been indicated, very little research has thus far been done on the effect of the presence of these foreign students on American students, but there is abundant testimony from both students and faculty of their influence. In a series of comments as to where their interests in foreign affairs were aroused, such comments from college students as the following appear regularly.

[14] *Ibid.*, p. 10.

The opportunity to discuss problems and cultural differences with college students from countries all over the world was the most significant influence on my attitudes.

In discussions with foreign students I have been able to get a much better idea of the feelings of other countries toward the United States, and more important, the reasons back of these feelings. My attitudes and beliefs about international questions have been changed and developed because of association with foreign students.

The one thing, excluding college courses, which has influenced me most with respect to foreign affairs has been my contact with foreign students.

An exploratory investigation in this field was made at Gustavus Adolphus College in Minnesota in 1954 in connection with the Carnegie Endowment program.[15] Nine out of ten faculty members, replying to a questionnaire, believed that there was an observable influence of foreign students on American students, even though Gustavus Adolphus had only 11 foreign students in a student body of 943. Over three-fifths of the upperclassmen in the same institution responded to a series of questions. About a fourth of the American students had had frequent contact with the foreign students; another 50 percent had occasional contacts; about a fourth had few contacts, and only 1 percent reported no contacts. Students reported that the contacts had increased their awareness of other countries (76 percent), added to their factual information (66 percent), influenced their choice of courses (7 percent) and of careers (12 percent). Most students had enjoyed the contacts and wished for more.

It seems likely that there will be little reduction during the years immediately ahead in the over-all number of foreign students in American colleges and universities. It seems likely, too, that they will be dispersed among American institutions on an even wider scale than at present. The desires and policies of the government departments and agencies concerned with

[15] I am indebted to Florence M. Fredricksen and Juul Altena of the Gustavus Adolphus faculty for making this survey and preparing the report based on it.

student exchange tend in this direction. The Eighty-third Congress included in its appropriation for the Department of State a specific endorsement of the wider distribution of government-aided exchangees among institutions throughout the country, and the Commission on Education and International Affairs of the American Council on Education has taken formal action to the same end. It seems likely, too, that on the basis both of continued experience and of the insights yielded by basic research now in progress, more effective selection, guidance, placement, and educational use of foreign students will become common. The work of the National Association of Foreign Student Advisers is a strong influence in this direction.

Sources of Students' Ideas about World Affairs

In analyzing members of the college community, it has been suggested that relatively few students take courses in international relations but that larger numbers value informal contact with specialists in the field. It has been suggested, too, that association of American students with foreign students is educationally powerful. It is obviously impossible to determine in general the exact pattern of influences on a campus which conditions most students' thinking about world affairs. But pertinent to our inquiry is an appraisal of where students think their ideas and attitudes about world cultures and international relations come from.

In the spring of 1954 a questionnaire, prepared in connection with the Carnegie Endowment's program, was distributed to selected seniors in fifty colleges and universities widely distributed throughout the United States. Included were rural and urban, and large and small institutions. Questionnaires were sent to individual faculty members in each institution who were requested to distribute them to a representative sampling of seniors about to graduate. There is no assurance that the selected seniors were equally typical or representative in all the institutions concerned, but the data accumulated from them are at least suggestive. The data indicate the nature of student interests and what influences students think have conditioned their ideas about world affairs. There is, of course, no assurance that students' thinking about the sources of their ideas is accurate. The data given below simply tabulate students' opinions.

While 1,500 student questionnaires were returned from the cooperating institutions, not all questions on each paper were filled out. Given a list of geographic areas and asked to check the one area most interesting and the one least interesting, a total of 711 students responded with the results indicated in Table 2. Greatest interest is shown in Europe, with the Soviet

TABLE 2

GEOGRAPHIC AREAS MOST AND LEAST INTERESTING TO 711
COLLEGE SENIORS IN 1954

GEOGRAPHIC AREA	MOST INTERESTING			LEAST INTERESTING		
	Men	Women	Total	Men	Women	Total
Europe	176	118	294	10	3	13
Middle East	27	21	48	34	22	56
South Asia	14	6	20	35	14	49
Southeast Asia	55	45	100	19	16	35
Soviet Area	74	56	130	7	2	9
Africa	13	10	23	174	106	280
Latin America	13	9	22	122	116	238
North America	48	26	74	19	12	31
Total	420	291	711	420	291	711

area and Asia ranking next; interest is extremely low in Africa and in Latin America. The data suggest what has been observed in other connections, regional differences in the foci of foreign interests. In the Southern states interest in Latin America looms large; on the West Coast, interest in Asia seems most marked; on the East Coast there is a certain preoccupation with Europe.

When asked to indicate the three topics they would most like to study if they were to take further work in international relations, 408 votes were cast for background of foreign policy, 338 for American-Soviet relations, 295 for the study of communism, 293 for cultural relations among nations, 246 for the United Nations system, 237 for international trade, 178 for technical development of backward areas, 177 for European union, 113 for nationalism, 103 for problems of the Pacific area, 97 for population pressures, 86 for questions of colonialism, and 51 for the British Commonwealth. It is, of course, quite possible that these represent ephemeral interests, but they suggest a range of topics apparently not adequately provided for in the program of courses which have been taken by a cross section of American college seniors. In view of the fact that in most institutions the study of international relations lies within political science, the interest expressed by students in economic, cultural, and sociological aspects of world relations needs particular attention.

Perhaps the most significant aspect of the survey arises from student estimates of the factors that have most influenced their ideas and attitudes about international affairs. A list of twenty possible sources of influence was placed before the seniors, and they were asked to indicate in rank order the five items on the list which in their opinion had been most influential on them as individuals. An arbitrary rating of these five on a scale of 5, 4, 3, 2, 1 was employed in tabulating the results. The data appear in Table 3,[16] indicating the total points assigned by 905 students to each of the twenty items, together with the average rating or score for each item, and a numerical indication of the degree of intensity accorded each item. As has been said, the data in Table 3 are based entirely on the subjective judgment of students; the actuality of influences on them may be very differ-

[16] For the tabulations and for aid in interpretation of these data I am indebted to Morris Berger, research assistant in the office of the president, Teachers College, Columbia University.

TABLE 3

RATING GIVEN 20 POSSIBLE INFLUENCES* AFFECTING OUTLOOK
ON WORLD AFFAIRS BY 905 COLLEGE SENIORS

Influence	Number of Students Including Item in Top 5	Total Number of Points Given Item	Average Rating†	Intensity Rating‡
1. Ideas and opinions of parents....	315	978	1.10	3.09
2. High school experience..........	73	229	.22	2.96
3. Church.......................	64	195	.20	3.18
4. Newspapers...................	562	1813	1.86	3.12
5. Newscasts....................	433	1295	1.23	2.81
6. Movies......................	102	200	.17	1.80
7. Magazines...................	480	1397	1.48	2.90
8. Books.......................	293	826	.96	2.84
9. Lectures....................	255	704	.89	2.74
10. Concerts....................	20	38	.03	1.45
11. Exhibits....................	11	20	.02	1.03
12. College courses taken...........	555	1965	2.36	3.55
13. Faculty members active in world affairs........................	127	409	.54	3.17
14. Military service...............	140	502	.41	2.99
15. Contacts with foreign students...	235	634	.71	2.69
16. Contacts with other foreign visitors	115	280	.31	2.43
17. Discussions and bull sessions with friends.......................	424	1123	1.21	2.60
18. Participation in student club activities......................	44	114	.12	2.50
19. Travel outside the United States..	152	571	.68	3.81
20. Vocational interests............	114	324	.34	2.71

* Each student rated the five most influential factors in a priority scale of 5, 4, 3, 2, 1.

† Average rating is calculated by dividing the total number of points allotted an item by the total number of students (905).

‡ Intensity rating is calculated by dividing the total number of points allotted an item by the number of students including the item in their top 5 influences.

ent from what they estimate those influences to be. But the data are suggestive for those who are concerned with planning such an informal collegiate program of education about world affairs as is advocated in this volume. The data support the thesis that all aspects and phases of the collegiate way of life should be considered in assaying and should be mobilized in planning college education about world affairs.

Purely on the basis of number of students including them in their priority lists, the chief influences are ranked as: (1) newspapers read, (2) college courses taken, (3) magazines read, (4) newscasts heard, (5) discussions engaged in with other students, and (6) parental ideas. Moreover, when the ratings are ranked on a scale running 5, 4, 3, 2, 1, the order is only slightly altered. In this ranking, college courses come first, followed, in order, by newspapers, magazines, newscasts, and student discussions. The lowest ranking items, beginning at the bottom, are exhibits, concerts, participation in student clubs, movies, church influences, and high school experiences. However, the data indicate a striking lack of unanimity among students; the two items most frequently included in the top five by students—newspapers and college classes—were each listed by only about three-fifths of the students. And conversely, no item was not included by at least a few students, though concerts and exhibits were chosen by very few indeed.

The survey failed to ascertain how many students had actually been subject to every one of the twenty influences. Thus such items as military service or travel may be experienced by only a few students, but may be powerful influences for those few. A rough measure of the intensity of student feeling about an influence is indicated in the last column of Table 3; the intensity rating indicates how high on the 5–1 scale an item was placed by only those who included the item on their list at all. In this situation, travel outside the United States was ranked highest by the 152 students who listed it at all. College courses held second rank, followed by the influence of contact outside of class with faculty members who were active in the actual conduct of world affairs. Church influences rise from a low average rating to a high intensity rating. In the top six influences are newspapers and parental ideas.

Table 4 analyzes still further the rating of influences given by 905 seniors, when they are grouped as (a) men or women,

(b) students from a college or from a larger university, and (c) students who had and who had not taken at least an introductory course in foreign policy or international relations.

TABLE 4

RANK ORDER OF TWENTY POSSIBLE INFLUENCES GIVEN BY 905 SENIORS CLASSIFIED AS TO MEN AND WOMEN, COLLEGE STUDENTS AND UNIVERSITY STUDENTS, AND STUDENTS WHO HAD AND WHO HAD NOT TAKEN A COURSE IN INTERNATIONAL RELATIONS

Influence	Men	Women	College	University	Course in IR	No Course in IR	Total
1. Ideas and opinions of parents........	7	3	6	6	7	6	6
2. High school experience.............	16	14	16	15	15	14	15
3. Church............	17	15	14	17	17	17	17
4. Newspapers........	1	2	2	1	2	1	2
5. Newscasts..........	4	6	7	3	6	2	4
6. Movies............	14	17	18	16	18	16	16
7. Magazines.........	3	5	3	4	3	4	3
8. Books.............	8	7	8	7	4	7	7
9. Lectures...........	10	8	4	10	8	9	8
10. Concerts..........	19	19	19	19	19	20	19
11. Exhibits...........	20	20	20	20	20	19	20
12. College courses taken	2	1	1	2	1	3	1
13. Faculty members active in world affairs..	12	11	11	13	10	15	12
14. Military service.....	6	18	13	8	12	10	11
15. Contacts with foreign students.......	11	9	10	9	11	8	9
16. Contacts with other foreign visitors......	15	12	12	14	14	13	14
17. Discussions and bull sessions with friends.	5	4	5	5	5	5	5
18. Participation in student club activities..	18	16	17	18	16	18	18
19. Travel outside the United States.......	9	10	9	11	9	11	10
20. Vocational interests..	13	13	15	12	13	12	13
Total number of persons involved.............	526	379	302	603	340	565	905

Of the 905 seniors who filled out the questionnaires, 526 were men and 379 were women. The top six influences recognized by each group include five identical items—newspapers, courses, magazines, discussions, and newscasts—though the rank order varies slightly. Men include military service in their top six items, though it ranks near the bottom of the list for women. To balance this, women accord third place in their list to parental ideas, while the men rate it seventh.

In spite of the fact that the terms "college" and "university" have overlapping meanings, the 905 seniors in the survey group were roughly classified as coming from colleges and as coming from universities. Three hundred and two students were in the former and 603 in the latter categories. Their six top-ranking influences are almost identical, except that college students accord lectures they have heard fourth place in their list, while it is tenth in the rank order given by university students. Newscasts, which rank third for university students, fall to seventh place for college students. Military service and vocational interests are given higher rating as influences by university students than by college students.

The questionnaire asked the 905 seniors whether they had taken, while in college, an introductory course in international relations. Three hundred and forty reported they had done so, while 565 indicated they had not. The replies provide data for faculty thought, for those who have not taken such courses rate the influence of the curriculum higher than do those who have taken introductory courses in international relations. In the top-ranking six items of those who have taken such courses appears the influence of parents, which is absent from the list of those who have not taken the courses; on the other hand, those who have not taken the courses put books in fourth place among the personal influences they recognize.

The main point, however, in the interpretation of these data is the range of influences which, in seniors' opinions, condition their outlook on world affairs. Every item on the list of twenty was rated in the top five by some students. If those who are interested in education about world affairs are to reach the great body of students, it is not sufficient to improve courses alone. Neither is it sufficient simply to improve library services, or to arrange more and better forums and public lectures. The same thing can be said for every other of the twenty items in the list. A wide-ranging, many-faceted program of collegiate education about world affairs, formal and informal, is essential if all students are to be reached.

Two other studies may be listed which lead to the same general conclusions. In 1954 the World University Service conducted a questionnaire survey involving 7,339 men and women students from 19 colleges and universities.[17] They were asked what influences had made them "aware of international affairs." Two influences were reported as predominant—(1) "books, radio, films, press," and (2) "courses of study." Following in order were "contacts with foreign students," "convocations or assemblies," "personal friend from another country," "church or religious campus organizations," "foreign language study," "organizations outside the college," "individual faculty influence," "travel or living abroad," and college organizations.

Similarly, a study of 275 students at Pennsylvania State University, made in connection with the Endowment's survey program, shows the wide diversity of approaches to student interest and understanding.[18] Table 5 reports degree of participation, attitudes toward, and estimates on the influence of 12 types of activities as reported by 275 students. The emphasis placed by the reporting group on contacts with foreign students, on lectures and forums, on courses about foreign cultures, and on films is significant, but the total range and pattern of activities is even more revealing. The college or university which seeks

[17] "Progress Report" (Mimeographed; New York: World University Service, May 1955).
[18] "A World-Affairs Survey of the Pennsylvania State University," op. cit., pp. 16–18.

TABLE 5

Responses of 275 Pennsylvania State University Seniors to a Questionnaire on Campus Activities Contributing to World Outlook

Campus Activity	Activities in Which Students Participated	Activities Contributing to Understanding of International Relations		Activities		Students Felt University Should Develop Activity More Fully
		Considerably	Slightly	Enjoyed	Disliked	
1. Took courses in which the subjects of other countries and peoples were stressed	143	86	19	41	10	85
2. Attended lectures, forums, discussion on international topics	143	77	11	47	8	91
3. Attended meetings of clubs or organizations primarily interested in world affairs and in fostering personal contacts between American and foreign students (International Relations Club, Cosmopolitan Club, etc.)	22	12	5	12	1	40
4. Made personal contacts with foreign students on an individual basis	179	118	13	113	0	70
5. Made personal contacts with foreign students through organized group meetings or social functions	103	58	14	54	0	102
6. Attended athletic events involving foreign teams	43	4	13	21	1	34
7. Read about other countries and peoples in books, magazines, and newspapers	240	117	25	55	1	15
8. Listened to radio or world television programs dealing with other countries and peoples	191	67	35	51	13	22
9. Saw foreign movies	211	41	86	92	2	55
10. Examined exhibits or bulletin board displays on international themes	128	6	48	10	5	17
11. Participated in activities in observance of Pan American Day, Columbus Day, or United Nations Week	33	3	10	4	1	13
12. Contributed to relief drives for needy countries	......	2	60	5	2	12

to educate all its students in respect to world relations needs to develop a program as broad as college life itself.

Campus Visitors

The members of the college have thus far been examined in terms of students and members of the faculty. In addition, what may be called temporary members of the college exercise considerable influence on the thinking of the college community. Their relations with both the younger and older "permanent" members of the college are predominantly of an informal, non-class nature, though their activities often reach the highest level of cocurricular enterprise.

Preceding pages have stressed the importance to education about world affairs of speakers and discussion leaders brought to the campus. These visitors, particularly if they approach the VIP level, may exert an influence quite out of proportion to the length of time they spend on the campus or even to the specific topic on which they speak. As "personalities in the news" they make an impression on the college community, leading to endless discussion and dissection of the personality as well as of the opinions of the visitor.

In this connection the governmental programs for bringing leaders from other countries for short-term visits should be considered. Many of these visiting leaders are routed to American colleges and universities. A substantial number of organized groups or study tours from abroad also find their way to campuses for periods of time. The burden of receiving these visitors and providing programs for them falls heavily on some campuses particularly exposed to their visits; it seems probable that the authorities responsible for the visits should make provision, financial and otherwise, for lightening the load of the colleges for visitors from abroad. But, whatever may be that decision, many visiting leaders can themselves be used to contribute to college life in the informal ways referred to in this volume. By lecturing, speaking before classes or clubs or faculties, advising on library and exhibit resources related to their own interests, being interviewed by student journalists, many of the short-time visitors may give to, as well as receive from, the institution.

The practice seems to be growing of inviting an outstanding person onto the campus not only to give a lecture but also to be a guest of the college for a longer period of time, associating informally with students and faculty. The Harvard and Yale houses as well as the guest houses of many institutions make provision for receiving and housing such visitors and for developing their visits as a stimulating part of the collegiate environment. An excellent program of this nature has been developed at Haverford College. Under a special foundation known as the Philips Visitors Program, Haverford brings men of consequence, largely people actively concerned with public life and international affairs, as guests of the college for a period of time, usually one to four weeks. Committees of faculty and students plan the visitor's schedule. He is likely to give one or two public lectures, to meet with and talk to classes on matters particularly within his competence, to visit various student groups informally, to dine with groups of students and faculty, to schedule individual interviews with selected students, to attend faculty meetings, and otherwise enter fully as a "resource person" into the life of the college. Every evidence indicates the arrangement is extraordinarily effective.

A report on the Haverford program, which was prepared by a student curriculum committee of the college in 1954, describes a visit to the college of Paul-Henri Spaak:

To take a typical example, we might examine the schedule of Paul-Henri Spaak, then President of the Council of Europe, while he was on campus for two weeks in the spring of 1952. Following the official program laid out by the college, he spent nine mornings in the Coop [college snack bar] between 10:00 and 11:00 in discussions with students, attended fifteen classes in seven different courses, participating in discussions related to his field, accompanied two field trips to Philadelphia—one to a factory, the other to a union meeting—and one trip to a farm in Lancaster County, spent three entire evenings in informal bull-sessions with those interested, under the direction of specially appointed students. In addition, enough time was set aside from these "formal" duties for conferences and completely spontaneous discussions in his living quarters.[19]

A somewhat similar program has been developed at Western College for Women in Oxford, Ohio. Visitors, largely from abroad, are invited to be guests of the college, participating in its life much as Spaak did at Haverford. At Western College visitors are in residence ordinarily for about a week out of each month of the academic year. Persons are invited who have a contribution to make to the enrichment of the college program, which emphasizes heavily and in sequence the cultures of other world areas.

The Haverford and Western College programs illustrate a general movement by which the life of a campus is enriched. Almost every college community is host periodically to "visiting firemen," but there are extreme variations in the degree with which the educative potentialities of such visits are cultivated. One proposal which has been advanced is that Foreign Service officers, on home assignment in the United States, should be given periods of time for campus visits. If developed with the care and ingenuity of those described above, such visits could be of great value both in bringing the experience and insight of foreign service to the campus and in reorienting the visitor, fresh from a sojourn abroad, into one of the most characteristic areas of American life.

One other development should be mentioned as affecting favorably a number of American academic communities. Organized in 1951, the American Universities Field Staff is a unique

---

[19] Haverford College Student Curriculum Committee, "The Philips Visitors Program," *Haverford Trends*, September 1954, p. 2.

link between certain American institutions and areas of the world which are ordinarily not adequately known. Under a small group of sponsoring colleges, a Field Staff of carefully selected area specialists spend somewhat more than half their time living in and studying the area of their specialization. The staff sends to the sponsors a considerable body of written analyses of developments in the area and serves as a point of reference for individual queries from sponsoring faculties. But, more important for the purposes of this discussion, the area specialists periodically visit their sponsoring campuses:

In addition to staff reports from the field, each sponsoring institution has the services of a number of returned AUFS men each year for campus visits of ten days or so each. Programs are devised locally to exploit the knowledge and experience of the visitors. Because each of them is already known for his writings from the field and perhaps from earlier visits, the campus steering committee can plan his schedule with understanding of the contributions he can make. While programs vary from campus to campus and from man to man, they regularly introduce AUFS visitors into interdisciplinary and departmental seminars, classes in the social sciences and humanities, foreign area study programs, faculty consultations, conferences, and other campus activities.[20]

Through arrangements such as these, campus life can be effectively enriched, surviving fragments of campus isolation eliminated, and the horizons of faculty and students alike broadened to encompass new areas.

Student-Faculty Relations

The basic point of view of this discussion is that one of the most significant aspects of college education is a way of life which encourages a wide range of contacts among members of the college. There are personnel resources in the college population, not limited to the specialists in international relations, which

[20] Phillips Talbot, "General Statement about the American Universities Field Staff" (Mimeographed; New York: American Universities Field Staff, 1954), p. 4.

may, and often do, exercise great influence on the ideas and attitudes about international affairs accepted by the individuals within that population. This influence is exerted in all aspects of college life, both in the classroom and on the campus. It has been argued, too, that these campus and classroom influences are being mutually strengthened by increased coordination between them. A reintegration of campus and classroom rests ultimately upon relations between students and faculty. This chapter has assumed the desirability of cooperative and stimulating relationships among all members of the college, young and old, permanent and temporary, if the full educative force of college life is to be harnessed.

In education about world affairs, as in all other fields, the experienced member of the college community is teaching in all his contacts with others. The faculty member with insight into other cultures, with international experience, with specialized knowledge is teaching students both in and out of his classroom. Much of his most influential and effective teaching is done in informal circumstances. The Swarthmore honors plan works well largely because of the intimate, friendly relation of students and instructors in informal seminars; the same quality characterizes all the college programs described in preceding chapters. Accounts written about great teachers emphasize out-of-class contacts fully as much as formal teaching in the classroom.[21]

The professor's role in the college community is more than that of a classroom teacher, or at least one must conclude that a college community cannot reach its highest educative level except as substantial numbers of the faculty assume the active role of senior members of the community. This is in no sense to suggest that the professor's role is that of a perpetual good

[21] See Houston Peterson (ed.), *Great Teachers: Portrayed by Those Who Studied Under Them* (New Brunswick, N.J.: Rutgers University Press, 1946).

fellow. The occasional faculty member who cultivates popularity by catering to students' tastes, who becomes a campus character under the delusion that his role is to be collegiate in the Hollywood sense, has little abiding influence. The professor without dignity is as bad in the community as the professor without learning. But the professor who is master of his subject and eager to communicate the findings of his specialization to others, who has demonstrated his competence in scholarship and in the application of that scholarship to the conduct of public affairs, and who recognizes and even enjoys a responsibility for making college a vitally educative experience for the whole campus community is the one whose influence permeates the entire life of the college. It is about such paragons that the great traditions of college life are built. Such men and women do not separate student life and faculty life into isolated sections; they merge the two into a more vital college life.

In the development of an integrated college life students have a responsibility commensurate with that of faculty members. The increasing maturity of college students has been described; with it has come a new role for students in college affairs. The danger lies, not so much in students returning to the relative juvenilism of the 1920's as in the tendency of some student groups to go it alone. If the present student movement developed into a youth movement, it would be bad both for higher education and ultimately for individuals.

It is not assumed here that students and faculty will always agree. Each group has interests legitimately its own. The fact, however, is that the college belongs to both groups and only as they recognize large areas of agreement and cooperate in joint tasks, each as appropriate taking the initiative, does college life reach its best level.

Conclusion

This chapter has brought together certain data and observations about the members of American colleges which lead to two basic conclusions—that both students and faculties are concerned and involved in international relations, and that among the members are many who constitute a rich resource for the further development of education about world affairs. Considering particularly the foreign students now resident on American campuses and the international experience and contact of a considerable proportion of faculty members, it seems obvious that members of the college have many opportunities, both formal and informal, for education about cultures other than their own, about foreign policy, and about world affairs. Whether the rich resources inherent in college members are utilized with maximum educational effectiveness is dependent upon some form of sensitive and imaginative social engineering within the institution.

———————————————*CHAPTER FOUR*

Student Activities

If [education] gives students the great themes of learning, it must also offer them some authentic participation in their own work. Education must not remain mere description, the learning of lessons, the performing of assigned, common chores. There must be some room for personal adventure and independent tasks in which a student can take creative pride. If colleges and universities try to civilize men with a body of liberal knowledge, they must also encourage the self-discovery and growth of persons in terms of what they can do.— Howard Foster Lowry, Modern Education and Human Values.

The individual is educated by the way he spends his time and by the situations into which he is put, or into which he accidentally falls.— Harold Taylor, "The Philosophical Foundations of General Education," Fifty-first Yearbook of the National Society for Education, Part I.

THE CONVICTION that "we live our way into thinking even more than we think our way into living" is the basic justification for extracurricular and cocurricular activities in the collegiate community and for the careful consideration of those activities as one aspect of collegiate education about world affairs. Student activities may be valid in themselves as good recreation, as a "release from overstudy," as experience in the management of group life, as athletic safeguards for health, but the chief reason why they are important in institutions of higher educa-

110

tion is determined by the contribution they make to the educational ends for which such institutions exist. These educational ends are paramountly intellectual, although not necessarily bookishly so. To develop to the full the intellectual talents which lie in those who go to college, to put trained talents into use, to make young adults capable of that wisdom which is "thought in action," it is necessary to develop a strong and exciting and worth-while program of college activities and to harness together harmoniously the out-of-class and in-class interests and enterprises of college life.

In the hortatory or nostalgic writing on student activities, it is common either to denounce them as time-wasters antagonistic to learning, or to glorify them as preparation for life, as character-forming, as training ground for leaders. Among those who have analyzed the campus community more objectively, it is common to defend activities as socially satisfying to undergraduates; activities are often justified in terms of their emotional value and the experience in creativity and in group living they provide. From the point of view of this volume, student activities may be worth while on character-making and emotional grounds, but their primary justification lies in the contribution they may make to intellectual and aesthetic development.

Obviously, not all campus activities make equal contribution to the intellectual development of students. A balanced campus life provides many recreational and social activities justifiable on grounds of their contribution to happiness, and with only minor overtones of intelligence-in-action. Some legitimate activities of the strenuous college life may be worth while simply as experience in group action, as training in leadership, as a form of civic apprenticeship. But many other activities carry a reasonable part of the intellectual weight of the institution. Among these latter activities may be discerned two major groupings—activities which seek to interest and inform and enrich the general body of students, and activities which are focused on the specialized interests of a few members of the college. In both these categories the purposes of education about world affairs may be served.

The undergraduate curriculum may be supplemented and enriched by relatively serious cultural out-of-class activities bearing on foreign and international matters, and the insights of those who are particularly interested in international relations may be deepened by well-chosen extracurricular enterprises. In preceding chapters certain of these activities were discussed in relation to the programs of college unions, college theaters, assembly halls, libraries, international houses, and other assets of the student-professor habitat. In the present chapter attention will be focused on student clubs and organizations, college journalism, and special campus events and observances in reference to their potentialities in education about world affairs.

Student Clubs

Student clubs are difficult to analyze in any systematic fashion, for their vitality is continually changing, their life span somewhat uncertain, and their records rarely written, or at least rarely preserved. On the one hand are many unorganized, relatively spontaneous groups or cliques of congenial students; it is in these groups that informal discussion is predominant. On the other hand, examination of any freshman handbook or of records in the offices of deans of students indicates how extensive and varied formally organized student groups are and how dear they are to the hearts of undergraduates.

The historical summaries in chapter 1 of this volume point out that student organizations, forbidden in colonial days, developed rapidly during the nineteenth century, sometimes as a reaction to the inert unreality of a traditional curriculum and sometimes as an escape into the excitements of student life.

There was the greatest variety among the activities, and many of them reflected temporary interests or the characteristic emphases of passing decades. At the University of Michigan, for example, almost six hundred organizations came into existence in the half-century following 1887, but only three-fifths of them survived. At Wittenberg College, three-fifths of the organizations created after 1881 were not in existence by 1931. But the number of active groups and the percentage of groups with serious intellectual interests increased. Ruth Strang, writing in *Group Activities in College and Secondary School,* summarized the trends in campus activities as follows:

The average number of extracurricular activities has increased. The highest mortality appears to be among music and literary societies, publications, oratory, debate, and dramatics, the lowest mortality among sororities, fraternities, honor societies, religious organizations, and student government. . . . Changes in the student activities in colleges reflect social changes which have paralleled the more obvious changes in the economic and social order.[1]

Among the organizations found on many campuses through most of the nineteenth century and on into the 1930's were literary societies. These societies gave zest and vigor to the learning process. Earnest praises them by saying that they "were probably more effective than the curriculum in fitting a man 'to perform justly, skilfully, and magnanimously all the offices both private and publick of Peace and War.' "[2] In meetings, usually held each fortnight, students engaged in formal debate, extemporaneous speaking, declamation, oratory, essay writing, and reading, all under the vigilant eye of elected student critics. Memory of these literary society meetings survived many years, enabling adults to quote for a lifetime passages of literature or points of view acquired there. The literary societies often

---

[1] Strang, *Group Activities in College and Secondary School* (New York: Harper & Bros., 1946), p. 83.

[2] Ernest P. Earnest, *Academic Procession: An Informal History of the American College, 1636 to 1953* (Indianapolis, Ind.: Bobbs-Merrill Co., 1953), p. 87.

built up their own libraries in an era when college libraries closed at five and the librarian worried if every book was not in its proper place on the shelves each night. Sometimes they maintained their own literary magazine. Examination of the programs of literary societies indicates how frequently and seriously they dealt with public issues of national policy and international welfare. It is in many ways unfortunate that in recent decades such societies have largely disappeared or have been converted to more exclusively recreational purposes. A renaissance of literary societies as a vital part of college life would be well worth the attention of faculty members, administrators, and student leaders interested in the quality of student experience, as well as of those concerned primarily with education in international relations.

On virtually every campus are to be found language clubs, existing partly to increase facility in a foreign tongue and in part to gain increased understanding of the culture for which the language is a vestibule. A report from Indiana University, for example, describes meetings and programs of the French Club, German Club, and Spanish Club which contribute substantially to the education of members in cultural diversities and contacts and in international questions. With the increasing emphasis in language instruction on speaking as well as reading, with the emphasis on language as a form of culture study, and with the appearance on many campuses of foreign students native to the tongue, the cultural effectiveness of language clubs seems to have increased.

Political clubs, heritage of the veterans on campus, and still reasonably well established among students in spite of an era of adult witch-hunting and repression, are involved in international relations to the same degree that international relations are involved in national politics. Departmental clubs in economics or business administration explore the field of international trade; history clubs examine the records of diplomacy;

political science and current affairs clubs deal with international organization and political issues; clubs organized around philosophical interests wrestle with value problems lying behind international controversies. There is no dearth of clubs concerned, in greater or less degree, with international matters; they abound on virtually every campus.

First examination of the varieties and vagaries of campus clubs gives an impression of confusion, of aimless activity for activity's sake, of overlapping, and perhaps of undue proliferation and expansion of clubs. Closer analysis, however, is likely to reveal on most campuses that the difficulty lies not in too many clubs but in too few students concerned with such activities. At the University of Minnesota,[3] for example, the directory of clubs in 1954 identified 399 organized, out-of-class student groups on the campus. But considerably less than a third of the university's students are involved in the clubs. Considering that there are 16,000 students enrolled at Minnesota, the long list of 399 clubs may be actually insufficient as aids for Minnesota students to "live their way into thinking." The few students who make a career of activities are not more a problem for educators than are the many students untouched by the club life of the community in which they live. In one of the earliest studies of club membership, made in 1924-25 by Chapin and Mehus, it was reported that 51.7 percent of freshman men and 43.3 percent of freshman women did not take part in any campus activities. Even in their senior year, 23.4 percent of the students, both men and women, had no share in organized campus life.[4] Porter Butts more recently has reported that only 3.5 percent of the total leisure time of all students goes into student

[3] "The University of Minnesota Directory of Student Organizations, 1954–55," compiled by the Student Activities Bureau, Office of the Dean of Students (Minneapolis: University of Minnesota, 1954).

[4] F. Stuart Chapin and O. M. Mehus, *Extra-Curricular Activities at the University of Minnesota* (Minneapolis: University of Minnesota Press, 1929).

activities, and that on the average for all types of institutions, between a third and a half of the students in college belong to an organized group of any kind.[5]

Among student clubs which have a primary concern with international relations and contacts are Cosmopolitan Clubs, International Relations Clubs, Collegiate Councils for the United Nations, nationality clubs, and organizations devoted to a particular interest such as world government or a geographic area or UNESCO. The Cosmopolitan Clubs have a long history as social organizations designed primarily to further contacts among students from different countries. In 1903 an "International Club" was founded at the University of Wisconsin,[6] to be followed a year later by a Cornell club having the same purposes and calling itself the Cosmopolitan Club. In 1906 a similar group was formed at Illinois, and in 1907 groups were organized at Purdue, Ohio State, Louisiana, and Chicago. In 1907 representatives of the groups met at Wisconsin and formed a national association. By 1909 the American Association was sending delegates to the Corda Fratres conferences in Europe, and in 1911, at Rome, the organizations were merged as the International Federation of Students. The international association did not survive World War I. After the war other campus groups took over some of the functions of the Cosmopolitan Clubs, but they continued to function on a moderate scale. Since World War II a number of the clubs have been revitalized, and to the social aspects of their programs have been added more systematic cultural studies. Where the clubs exist they meet a need for foreign students; their chief problems are those of attracting suitable American students in good numbers, and

[5] Butts, "The State of the College Union: The Social and Educational Goals of the Campus Center," *Journal of Higher Education,* February 1951, p. 83.

[6] The International Relations Club at Wisconsin now forms a unit of the Wisconsin Union and carries on an active program. See *The International Club of the University of Wisconsin: 50 Years of World Fellowship,* a booklet published in 1953 by the International Club of the Wisconsin Union.

their chief advantages lie in the services often given them by the offices of foreign student advisers.

One of the student associations most active today in the field of international relations is the Collegiate Council for the United Nations. Organized in 1946 under the sponsorship of the American Association for the United Nations, its purposes are:

1. To stimulate an understanding of the purpose, scope, and functions of the United Nations on the campus and in the community.

2. To give expression to student opinion on the United Nations on a national level.

3. To coordinate and stimulate United Nations activities and programs on individual campuses and in the regional areas throughout the United States.[7]

The council holds an institute each spring near the headquarters of the United Nations at which chosen representatives from campuses all over the country study United Nations affairs and meet with leaders from the Secretariat and from national delegations. This intensive week of consultation provides an extraordinary experience for participants. The council organizes model United Nations assemblies, often on a regional basis, and holds an annual convention for student delegates.

Its major work, however, is done in the individual councils which, in 1955, existed on 335 campuses. Club members meet regularly for the discussion of current United Nations affairs, often taking positions on issues and making those positions known to the government through the national association. The councils work ordinarily in close relation with a faculty adviser and undertake campaigns and drives for the purpose of interesting and informing the whole college community on the field of their special interest. The American Collegiate Council, moreover, works closely with student groups in other countries through the World Federation of United Nations Associations.

[7] *Constitution* of the Collegiate Council for the United Nations. See also "A U.N. Handbook for You: Campus Programming Suggestions for C.C.U.N. Groups" (Mimeographed; New York: Collegiate Council for the United Nations, 1954).

International Relations Clubs: a Case Study

Among the oldest student organizations directly concerned with world affairs are the International Relations Clubs. Since a considerable part of their records are available, and a recent study of their operations has been made, they may be presented in more detail as a case study of club activity, and as the basis for analysis of problems and issues arising about clubs in general.

Just prior to the outbreak of World War I Norman Angell and Stephen Duggan became interested in organizing student groups to discuss international relations. Under the impetus of Angell's book, *The Great Illusion*, the movement gained headway. In 1912-13 discussion groups were organized at Cornell, Columbia, and elsewhere. Known as International Polity Clubs, they had phenomenal growth as a result of the outbreak of war in Europe. By the spring of 1915 there were thirty-eight such groups on American campuses.

The movement ebbed for a time, but after World War I it gained renewed headway. In 1920 the clubs became known as International Relations Clubs, and in 1924, under a plan developed by Duggan and Nicholas Murray Butler, the Carnegie Endowment for International Peace assumed the expense and secretarial responsibility involved in stimulating and aiding the clubs. Work with the International Relations Clubs continued as an aspect of the Endowment's regular program for thirty years. By 1940 almost eight hundred such clubs were in existence in the United States and Canada; some six hundred of these survived the war and early postwar years.

An article in the *Educational Forum* in 1950 reported:

These student clubs were serious study groups. Each was under the sponsorship of a faculty sponsor. Regular meetings were held monthly or semimonthly at which questions of international relations were discussed. Students prepared papers, heard lectures, engaged in debates, discussed the world issues of the day. To each club the

Carnegie Endowment sent each semester a packet of four or five books on varied aspects of world affairs, for it was a period when college libraries were not themselves purchasing widely in the field. The offices of the Carnegie Endowment provided a secretariat for the clubs; an Endowment staff member maintained contact with the clubs by correspondence and by visiting. . . . The importance of the clubs rested not on idle interest among students. The clubs opened up a field for study which was not opened by many standard curricula. The clubs served almost a vocational need, for in them a good many young men and women were stimulated toward careers in international service. . . . The roster of former club members now serving the United States government and the United Nations is impressive.[8]

After the difficulties of the war period the clubs gained vitality through the arrival of veterans on the campus, bringing extensive interest in the realistic, thoughtful consideration of international issues. Under veterans' leadership, an Association of International Relations Clubs was organized in 1948. In time, with financial aid from the Endowment, an executive secretary was employed, and in 1954 arrangements were completed for sponsorship of the Association of International Relations Clubs by the Foreign Policy Association. The clubs are now to be found on approximately seven hundred campuses in the United States and Canada, independently carrying on their own programs, though interrelated through their association and sponsored by the Foreign Policy Association. Many regional meetings and state or metropolitan meetings of the clubs are held, and an annual convention of representatives of the clubs attracts several hundred students to a program ordinarily of high intellectual level.

A recent statement from the Executive Board of the Association of International Relations Clubs (AIRC), composed of representatives of students and faculty advisers and of the Foreign Policy Association, says:

International Relations Clubs are student organizations, primarily serious in character, which help to develop student interest and under-

[8] Howard E. Wilson, "International Relations Clubs," *Educational Forum*, May 1950, pp. 403–4.

standing in the international conditions of our time. Through study and program activities, the clubs serve as educative instruments helping to inform a larger audience both on the campus and in the community.

The AIRC does not espouse any particular solutions to international questions, but does seek, through program aids sent to individual clubs, to encourage study and understanding of foreign-policy issues.

The AIRC, as the national coordinating office: maintains contact with each local club; maintains an information service for club program planning; calls an annual national conference; encourages and aids regional conferences; sends out suggested program and discussion aids; issues the monthly *AIRC Newsletter*, maintains a representative on the United States National Commission for UNESCO; has observer status on the Young Adult Council; is a member of the National Consultative Committee of World University Service.[9]

In 1954, as a part of the Endowment's program on universities and world affairs, a survey was made of the problems and activities of International Relations Clubs. An extensive questionnaire was mailed to 655 clubs which yielded usable responses from 233, or 35.5 percent, of the institutions. Replies came from 42 of the 48 states, the District of Columbia, and two provinces of Canada. Size of college or university seems to have little influence on the actual existence of clubs, though it affects markedly the character of club programs. The clubs are distributed among institutions of different sizes in almost the same proportion as the distribution in size categories of the total number of institutions themselves. About 2.7 percent of the total group of registrants in the 203 four-year colleges surveyed hold formal membership in the International Relations Clubs, though a considerably larger percentage attend club meetings from time to time. More upperclassmen than underclassmen are enrolled as members; approximately twice as many seniors as freshmen are in the clubs. The number of men and women is approximately equal. About a tenth of the club members are

[9] Mimeographed statement; see also William C. Gibbons, "A Handbook for International Relations Clubs" (New York: Association of International Relations Clubs, 1954).

foreign students, and less than a twentieth, in 1954, were veterans. About half of all the 7,500 club members reported in 203 four-year colleges or universities are majoring in the social sciences; of the other half, two-fifths are in the humanities, two-fifths in professional or preprofessional training, and one-fifth in the natural sciences.

All of the clubs regard themselves as primarily informal study and discussion groups, and their regular meetings ordinarily constitute their chief activity. Of 233 clubs—203 in four-year and 30 in two-year institutions—26 hold weekly meetings, 97 fortnightly, 87 monthly, and the others "on call." The form of club programs is indicated in Table 6.

TABLE 6

TYPES OF MEETINGS HELD BY 233 INTERNATIONAL
RELATIONS CLUBS IN 1954

Type of Program	Frequently	Occasionally	Seldom	Never	No Reply
Guest speaker	94	113	19	0	7
Business session	94	81	33	11	14
Panel forum	75	100	32	14	12
Member speaker	69	99	30	12	23
Social gathering	27	110	44	32	21
Film showing	24	85	62	35	27
Debate	23	46	69	60	35
Slide showing	16	59	51	69	38
Field trip	7	47	45	87	46
Book review	5	34	44	107	43

The extent to which lectures are involved in club programs should be pointed out, particularly in view of the influence of lectures on student thinking which has been reported earlier. It should be indicated, too, that much of the club business referred to in Item 2 of the table is concerned with special events or drives or other enterprises by which the total campus and sometimes the larger community as well can be involved in world affairs matters.

The substantive character of topics and issues discussed or lectured about in club meetings is shown in Table 7. Issues

TABLE 7

ASPECTS OF INTERNATIONAL RELATIONS DEALT WITH IN THE PROGRAMS OF 233 INTERNATIONAL RELATIONS CLUBS IN 1954

Aspects	Frequently	Occasionally	Seldom	Never	No Reply
Foreign policy questions.........	157	49	12	4	11
Political issues.......	150	60	10	3	10
Current events......	146	55	14	6	8
Economic issues.....	72	102	27	15	17
Cultural issues.......	58	99	39	13	24
Area studies.........	58	66	42	29	38
Historical analysis...	31	76	45	38	43
Geographic influences	27	80	54	31	41
Population problems.	17	63	68	45	40

of foreign policy, political issues, and current events seem to predominate in the programs. Economic matters receive considerable attention, and cultural relations somewhat less. Historical and geographic factors, presumably more adequately cared for in ordinary courses, are not characteristically popular club areas of interest.

While all the clubs emphasize, both in their stated objectives and in their program reports, that they exist primarily for the interest and enlightenment of their own members, most of the clubs are also concerned with arousing interest in international affairs for a larger audience. Some three-fourths of the reporting group of clubs indicate that they are active in campus and community enterprises designed to present significant information to the public. Clubs open many of their meetings to other students, often at the request of and with the financial support of the college administration; they sponsor lectures or forums for the campus and community; they prepare articles on world affairs for the student newspaper; they operate a speakers' bureau through which club members and many foreign students appear as speakers for other organizations. Among the 233 colleges included in the survey, 106 maintain a campus bulletin board for the display of items bearing on international news; 87 sponsor public lecture series; 82 prepare feature articles for the campus newspaper; 58 broadcast radio programs on the local station; 17 maintain speakers bureaus; and 15 participate in television programs.

Factors Affecting Club Vitality

A number of factors about special-interest clubs on campus appear as important, not only in the case study of the International Relations Clubs, but in connection with all special-interest undergraduate clubs and societies. The first factor is the relationship which an individual club has to the network of clubs on the campus. Ordinarily in a college, a club can be organized fairly simply; the initiative rests with students; by securing a faculty sponsor and the approval of the dean's office or of the general student association, a club may come into existence. The club then operates within a network of organized-group, campus relations which ultimately determine its status and prestige in college life. Clubs compete with other clubs for student time and attention and support. On a few campuses surveyed, for example, the International Relations Club seems to be an eddy in the current of student life, outside the main channel of student affairs; in some cases such a club has an organic relationship with the student association and performs functions in its field for the whole student body; in most institutions each club tends to operate independently, cooperating on occasion with other organizations, sometimes competing with them, occasionally called upon by the administration for special tasks. Viewed sociologically, one has too frequently the impression that clubs are caught in a campus life which is unplanned, uncoordinated, unstructured. While freedom and initiative are vital to campus welfare, the structural chaos of life on many campuses is actually inimical to collegiate education. A degree of structuring and planning and coordination would enhance the educative value of clubs, including the special-interest clubs dealing with international relations.

A central factor in determining the vitality and validity of a special-interest club is the faculty adviser. It is the faculty adviser who provides continuity in club development. A major reason why International Relations Clubs have thrived on campuses through four decades, for example, is the interest taken in them by faculty advisers. The best advisers do not act simply as *pro forma* sponsors, but as full partners in organizing clubs and developing their programs. As Williamson has pointed out, "To utilize the extracurriculum as a teaching device . . . we must rid ourselves of the dictum of the sanctity of students' complete and autonomous control of their own affairs." [10] In effecting a measured balance between study and action, the wisdom of mature faculty members is paramountly significant. Clubs which have been exclusively, even belligerently, student-controlled or have been neglected by overretiring and reluctant faculty members have tended to be ephemeral, and at the same time clubs which have been faculty-dominated have tended to reach but few students and to have little prestige in the structure and mores of campus life.

It is in the friendly, cooperative, counseling, and stimulating relationship of older and younger members of the college that the strength of special-interest clubs lies. Both faculty adviser and students have to exercise initiative, and feel free in doing so, if a club is to be successful. The role of a faculty counselor is not easy; it requires certain personality qualities, infinite tact

[10] E. G. Williamson, "The Extracurriculum and General Education," *General Education,* Fifty-first Yearbook of the National Society for the Study of Education, Part I (Chicago: University of Chicago Press, 1952), p. 242.

and patience. Unfortunately, the role is not well recognized in the ordinary priorities of academic advancement. The practice of turning club-counseling posts over to members of the department least able to resist the assignment of an onerous, unrewarded chore to be done for a time is understandable but is to be condemned on all educational grounds. Specialists in international relations genuinely concerned either with raising the level of educational understanding on the campus as a whole or in providing enriching, informal education for those especially interested in international relations, will find it particularly worth while to foster and counsel and aid student clubs concerned with the field.

Another matter affecting the vigor and effectiveness of clubs, including those particularly interested in international affairs, is that of the relations among similar clubs on different campuses. The history of the International Relations Clubs again illustrates the importance of intercampus contacts. These clubs were first organized in local, often in state, then in regional associations and finally in a national association. In the survey conducted in 1954 and in extensive correspondence with club officers and advisers, the desire of clubs on individual campuses to avoid isolation has been strongly expressed. Meetings of students from several campuses at which students who share interests in international relations find mutual stimulation are often positive stimuli for the work of individual clubs.

Closely related to intercampus contacts for clubs is their relationship to adult, off-campus agencies. This matter is often one of controversy, but there seems little doubt that, in general, campus special-interest clubs profit from such contact. Again taking the International Relations Clubs as examples, the services rendered them by the Carnegie Endowment for three decades and now rendered by the Foreign Policy Association were and are basic to the growth and development of individual clubs. Outside sponsorship by a respected and responsible agency is attractive to many faculty advisers; the stimulation and counsel from an outside sponsor or secretariat are fully as helpful to clubs as are any material services or financial aid they may receive. The outside contact gives an element of reality to academia which students generally cherish so long as it does not involve domination. The services of the American Association for the United Nations to the Collegiate Councils for the United Nations are extremely important to the councils. Many campus groups find similar sponsorship and service in church organizations or in the Young Men's and Women's Christian Associations.

Off-campus, nonacademic relationships for campus clubs bring problems as well as stimulation and service. Outside propaganda agencies, more or less masked, may establish or serve student groups on campus for undesirable ends. In the history of American student organizations instances may be found of undesirable, sometimes undercover, infiltrations into campus life. These dangers enhance the importance of experienced faculty advisers for special-interest clubs, and of such administrative formulations and clarifications of policy toward college life as are described later in this volume. The university needs to set up the machinery by which the dangers of outside sponsorship are minimized and the advantages are maximized. The task of an outside sponsor is not unlike that of the faculty adviser. It needs to encourage and counsel without dominating, to facilitate learning and the interchange of data without propagandizing, to be alert in providing aids and services without reducing the initiative and responsibility of individual clubs.

It should be pointed out that many campus clubs seek a program which is a combination of study and action. In situations where clubs are simply extensions of the classroom occupations of study and learning, they do not seem to be adequately vital. And where students rush into action, even from the best of motives, without careful thought and study, they become ridiculous from the viewpoint of all that a university stands for.

The veterans on campus after World War II for the most part were interested in combining serious study of international matters with doing something about the situation, and this interest seems to continue as a part of their heritage to the college. The enormous activity of students in raising money and materials for foreign relief is an expression of their desire for action. So also is the acceptance of student-group representatives on such public or semiofficial groups as the Citizens Committee for United Nations Day or the United States National Commission for UNESCO. The means and procedures of citizen participation in the formation of public opinion and policy at the adult level would seem to be legitimate areas of practice—almost apprenticeship—for many student groups.

College Journalism

One of the student activities with high prestige and educative potential on virtually all American campuses is student journalism. Often related to the formal curriculum in journalism or in the English Department, sometimes serving the whole town as well as the campus, the student newspaper is a vital part of college life. The college newspaper staff is one of the most active groups on most campuses, and its work has considerable value for informal campus education about world affairs. Its staff ordinarily attracts able students; it is commonly the most widely and consistently read newspaper on the campus. The newspaper can alert students to facets of world affairs and add substantially to their sensitivities and understandings in this area. Examined from the point of view of what they present about international relations, the college newspapers stand up well—stand up better, as a matter of fact, than do many local newspapers for general citizens. The campus newspaper of the University of British Columbia published twenty editorials on international issues in one recent year; the daily paper of

Indiana University opened its columns to Iranian and British students for vigorous discussion of the Iranian oil question; the report from Brown University on its survey of resources and activities bearing on world affairs says:

The undergraduate newspapers, the *Brown Daily Herald* and the *Pembroke Record*, seek to keep the student body informed on current international developments. Their columns frequently contain items such as: news reports and feature articles; articles by American students who have been abroad or letters from students who are abroad; letters from students on their native lands; articles by, or interviews with, foreign students now at the University.[11]

In connection with the survey program of the Carnegie Endowment, an informal analysis of a random group of college papers published on thirty-two campuses during the first ten days of December 1954 was made. Small and large, rural and urban institutions were included in the surveyed group. Some of the larger institutions issued more than one publication during the survey period; two of the papers examined—the *Daily Iowan* and the *Columbia Missourian*—serve entire communities and are virtually a part of the public press. Geographical location, size of institution, and frequency of publication of the journals seem to have little to do with coverage of matters having international implications. The seven student papers of the College of the City of New York for December 1–10, 1954, contained less material bearing on world affairs than did the publications of Pennsylvania State University or Indiana University. On the other hand, New York University's five student publications for the same period contained a good deal on international affairs. The newspaper of only one of the thirty-two colleges surveyed included no item whatever on world affairs for the period analyzed.

[11] "Brown University and World Affairs," *Universities and World Affairs,* Document No. 50 (Mimeographed; New York: Carnegie Endowment for International Peace, 1954), p. 13.

The college papers which are issued most frequently tend to be members of the professional press services and to carry some wire stories of major current events in world affairs. Newspapers belonging to the Associated College Press receive and frequently carry stories of international reference having particular interest to colleges. Thus, for example, during the period surveyed this press service emphasized the controversy over whether the Military and Naval Academy students were to be allowed to debate on the topic of Red China's admission to the United Nations. Almost all college papers gave substantial attention to this topic both in news stories and in editorials. College newspapers carry many items concerning campus events dealing with world affairs, regardless of whether they are members of the news services. In almost every instance the college papers feature local items as their lead stories; the wire service stories are usually given second or third billing, and ordinarily relatively little space.

Among the local items having some relation to international matters, stories about foreign students appear most frequently. Many of the papers examined ran personal interviews with foreign students as regular features. These human-interest stories are apparently very widely read; as one observer noted, college newspaper attention to the "postwar influx of foreign minds in foreign bodies has created on the college campus an awareness of life beyond our shores that is quite different from the academic knowledge of the color of Pakistan on even the latest map." Reports on guest lectures on world relations and on visiting foreign artists rank second to foreign students in amount of space and interest allotted in college papers. Every college paper except one gave space during the ten-day period analyzed to fairly extensive news reports on lectures, concerts, art exhibits, or foreign visitors. This reportage varied from lead stories on the visit of London's Old Vic to the campus at Michigan State University to the announcement of a local language club in another institution playing host to a minor consular official.[12]

Choosing at random an issue of the *Chicago Maroon* for May 6, 1955, a description of its content illustrates the range and character of college journalism as a force in education about world affairs. The *Maroon*, published weekly, is read by virtually all the undergraduates and most of the graduates in the student body at the University of Chicago. The selected issue of the *Maroon* is 12 pages long, of tabloid size. Its 12 pages contain space for 900 column inches of print; of these 474 inches are used for news stories, editorials, and announcements, while 426 inches are used for advertising. Eight column inches are given to a report on a lecture by the Ambassador from the Netherlands, speaking on "The Dutch View of the World Situation Today." Half as much space announces a lecture to be given by a visiting scholar from India on "Abiding Contrasts between Hinduism and Christianity," and six inches are given to announcing the award of a prize to a graduate student in the university for a volume on Benjamin Franklin's concept of foreign policy. Eighteen column inches are given to a story on a project for studying the Japanese language under way by a group of University of Chicago students. Three inches announce a coming presentation of international folk music, four inches describe a series of international film showings at International House, and 21 inches deal with local staging of plays by Sean O'Casey, Franz Kafka, and Luigi Pirandello. Twelve column inches report an address by a visiting senator on "The Reality of Disarmament." All in all, some 86 column inches, almost 10 percent of the total space, are more or less directly related to international matters, and 24 inches, a little less than 3 percent, are directly on world affairs. It could not be contended that these materials constitute a program of education about

[12] For analysis of these college newspapers I am indebted to Mr. Jack Dawley.

world affairs, but it is obvious, nevertheless, that readers of the *Maroon* are regularly alerted to a considerable range of international matters.

Those who are concerned with campus-wide orientation of students to a world point of view need to consider the possibilities in student journalism more than is ordinarily done at present. Specific training of journalists in international matters may well be as important at the student level as at the adult level; a contribution toward professional excellence in this field could well be made through undergraduate cocurricular experience. Periodic content analysis of student publications made cooperatively by journalists and those concerned with international relations could lead to further improvements in treatment of world affairs in the student papers. Mention has already been made of the articles contributed to journals by members of the Collegiate Councils for the United Nations and by the International Relations Clubs; other campus resources for useful journalistic material may well be tapped.

Other Activities

As was indicated in the early paragraphs of this chapter, student activities which have a high potential intellectual content include much more than student clubs and college journalism. Some of the activities such as student travel and student participation in college government will be discussed in later chapters, but a number of types of activities deserve mention here.

Debating has from time immemorial been an occupation of college life. College unions originated in debating societies; debating was a major part of the programs of literary societies. In recent decades it seems to have suffered a decline, although a national debating league exists which holds annual series of debates on a chosen topic. Examination of these topics shows that many of them in recent years have dealt with some phase of international relations. An analysis of the study students undertake, either to make the debate team or to win its victories, indicates that the preparation for debate is an intense intellectual exercise.

Within the last few years some indications have appeared of a reviving interest in debate. Visits of the Oxford debating team to many American campuses have stimulated interest. The Wisconsin Union has deliberately sought to popularize debate, in part by arranging for audience participation in the selection of winners. The West Point debating team's annual series of debates have demonstrated high standards of performance on many campuses. It is possible that even greater attention to debate will come, and that it can be organized as an effective cocurricular activity in education about world affairs.

Another type of student activity, originating in international problems and with a long record of achievement, is the program of World University Service. World University Service is not an individual membership organization with clubs on campuses; it is a complex structure of national and international committees and sponsors composed of students and adults. To its activities large numbers of students on campuses throughout much of the world give time and thought and money. Organized primarily as a relief agency, the World University Service has taken on additional functions and is an educative force of consequence.

In 1920, in war-ravaged Vienna, a representative of the World Student Christian Federation organized a movement of relief and rehabilitation for university students and faculty. The movement appealed to university communities in economically more advantaged areas and, within months, the General Committee of the World Student Christian Federation set up an autonomous unit known as European Student Relief. For five years this unit conducted an active campaign for funds and material from

university communities for the use of needy students and professors. Enormous relief was given to areas suffering from war
damage or natural catastrophes, and in the process a network
of relations among humanitarian-minded students throughout
the world was created. In 1926 this led to the creation of an
independent international organization incorporated under Swiss
law as International Student Service (ISS), with headquarters
at Geneva.

From then until the Second World War, the ISS continued to
stimulate service by members of the university community for members of that community. Relief schemes were operated in Bulgaria
after the earthquake, in China during the Sino-Japanese war, and
for the benefit of university refugees from Germany and Austria.
International study tours, seminars and work camps were arranged.
International conferences were held in Europe and America, bringing
together members of the university community for exchanges of
views and information on topics such as self-help schemes, student
health, anti-Semitism, student journalism, training of teachers, selection of students, and disarmament.[13]

In a real sense, World University Service had grown into an
important part of the international relations of universities themselves and had done so on the basis of cooperative action among
both faculties and students.

During World War II and the immediate postwar years,
International Student Service again concentrated heavily on
relief work. It became the operating agency for a program of
World Student Relief sponsored by the service itself and by
international associations of Protestant and Catholic and Jewish
students and by the International Union of Students. Operating
on a nondiscriminating policy and with years of experience
behind it, World Student Relief raised and distributed millions
of dollars in the decade of the 1940's.

In 1951 the temporary relief agency was disbanded, and
International Student Service changed its name to World Uni-

[13] British Cooperating Committee of World University Service, *WUS
Yearbook: 1955* (London: World University Service, 1953), pp. 11–12.

versity Service (WUS). With international headquarters in Geneva, it has sponsoring committees in some forty countries. The American committee, composed of students and adults, maintains a national headquarters in New York and staff officers in each region of the United States. Working cooperatively with student organizations such as those already mentioned and with student government groups, World University Service now raises funds for relief, convenes conferences and institutes, aids worthy student projects of an international character, and carries on research concerning university community life.

It is impossible to say to what extent the campus activities of World University Service have influenced student ideas and attitudes about world affairs, but there is evidence that its relief campaigns have sensitized many students to international matters. As has already been pointed out, the program of WUS provides for action as well as thoughtfulness and high motive, and it has appealed tremendously to large groups of students. As a force for educating a campus about world affairs, it warrants support and careful coordination with other student activities.

Special Campus Events

Consideration either of the program activities of student clubs or of campus life as reported in student newspapers brings into view a wide variety of special events on campuses which have cocurricular significance in education about world affairs. Many of these events are cherished in the traditions and mores of an institution. Such events are supported by both students and faculty; many administrators would agree with the president of Colby College when he says, ". . . next to the curriculum itself, I would place what might be called special devices for arousing an interest in the curriculum or making it an object of lively attention." [14] A great many colleges and universities recognize United Nations Day on October 24 as an occasion for informing and educating both students and faculty through special assemblies or convocations, lectures, forums, pageants, and exhibits. The event is sometimes recognized as United Nations Week. A report from Indiana University, for example, indicates that:

It has become traditional for the University to participate in the celebration of United Nations Week. A coordinator is customarily appointed by the Vice-President and Dean of Student Affairs and this coordinator attempts to utilize facilities to arouse interest in international affairs. For the United Nations Week this year, letters were sent to members of the faculty urging them to entertain, if possible, foreign students in their home some time during the week; the Bookstore and the Library arranged excellent displays; posters were placed on bulletin boards throughout the campus; the Union Building carried out a decoration theme of United Nations flags and featured a foreign dish [at the] cafeteria daily as well as included in the menu at the Union Club a foreign special each day. United Nations films were shown by the Audio-Visual Aids Department and spot broadcasts were given throughout the week by the University station. Foreign students participated on television programs and were guests for dinner during the week at a number of fraternity and sorority houses. The *Daily Student* had a number of editorials during United Nations Week pointing up the celebration.[15]

Observance is sometimes made of Pan-American Day, Human Rights Day, International Students Day, or occasionally a festival day of another country in which the campus is particularly interested. Some of these observances have high educational value, combining emotional stimulus with intellectual analysis. It is desirable for every institution of higher education to appraise its activities of this character, and to give careful thought to the effective developments of such observances as are particularly appropriate.

[14] "President's Report" (Waterville, Maine: Colby College, December 1954), p. 7.
[15] "Indiana University in World Affairs," *Universities and World Affairs*, Document No. 26 (Mimeographed; New York: Carnegie Endowment for International Peace, 1953), p. 19.

A number of ambitious special events may illustrate possibilities along these lines. Since 1944 Michigan State University, for example, has held an International Festival each spring.[16] The first festival was unpretentious and limited to a small group of foreign students and their campus friends, but it has since grown into a major educational and social enterprise. The eleventh annual festival in 1955 was an all-day affair under the direction of the Dean of Students' Office in cooperation with the International Club, Student Government, Spartan Women's League, Michigan State College Veterans' Association, Young Women's and Young Men's Christian Associations, and Extension Women's Club. It involved presentation of national dances and music, exhibits of national handicrafts and materials on cultural contacts, lectures and discussions; it attracted some thirteen thousand visitors, both students and townspeople. It appears to be thoroughly established as an item in the university's way of life, and to help shape the attitudes toward other cultures held by students.

The survey conducted in connection with the Carnegie Endowment program at the State College of Washington in Pullman reports that:

An annual week-long International Festival presents a program in the area of world affairs. Foreign students lead a series of discussions in various student residences, and several social functions and an international student show emphasizing international motifs take place. Widespread publicity is given the event, and foreign students from other colleges and universities in the area are brought to the campus to participate. Likewise, high school seniors from all schools of the state are invited to attend, and generally from one hundred to two hundred high school students are included in the various activities of the festival.[17]

[16] "Michigan State College and World Affairs," *Universities and World Affairs,* Document No. 69 (Mimeographed; New York: Carnegie Endowment for International Peace, 1954), pp. 21–22.

[17] "State College of Washington, Final Report of the World Affairs Survey Committee," *Universities and World Affairs,* Document No. 27 (Mimeographed; New York: Carnegie Endowment for International Peace, 1953), p. 24.

One of the most striking annual campus events connected with world affairs is the United Nations Week held each spring at the University of Colorado. During the week the entire campus is animated by something of the same spirit which characterized the Chautauqua movement at its height. An intensive program of public lectures and forums is arranged in which key persons in the field of international relations and officials from the United States Department of State and the United Nations participate. Libraries and museums arrange exhibits. Individual classes utilize pertinent materials and topics concerning the United Nations program, and the general lectures become something of a common element in the entire curriculum. Student clubs arrange special meetings for the week, emphasizing their particular interests in the United Nations. The celebration has taken on the character of a university tradition. It requires close cooperation of faculty and student groups. There is every evidence of its educational effectiveness.

An event widely popular among American students is a model session of the United Nations General Assembly or the Security Council or the Economic and Social Council. Started at Syracuse University in the days of the League of Nations, the model assemblies have repeatedly demonstrated their educational effectiveness. Ordinarily regional in character, they involve many colleges and require elaborate preparation by students. At the Fifth Model Assembly of colleges and universities on the West Coast, for example, representatives from more than seventy institutions convened at San Francisco State College in May 1955. Detailed preparation, in which each college group played the part of a particular nation, involved the formulation and submission of resolutions relating to specific predetermined issues. The model assembly, convening in the historic hall where the United Nation's Charter was signed, conducted business under Assembly rules of procedure and heard addresses by representatives of the United Nations itself. Student groups worked in close cooperation with faculty advisers, and evidence from both sources attests the enterprise as serious, challenging, and valid. When a model assembly has sufficient proportions and adequate preparation, it may become a major event in the education of those who participate in it.

An outstanding conference for students dealing with questions of foreign policy and international relations is convened annually at West Point. The purposes of this Student Conference on United States Affairs (SCUSA) are: (1) to hold an informative examination and discussion of a particular topic selected for the conference, (2) "to provide an outstanding representation of college students with an appreciation of the complexities of government policy formulation," and (3) "to broaden students' contact with their contemporaries in an academic endeavor." [18] The sixth such conference, held in December 1954, dealt with "The National Security Policy of the United States"; to it came 150 carefully selected and able students from 63 colleges and universities, who took part in the proceedings as speakers, round-table chairmen, advisers, observers, and participants in the discussion. A distinguished group of experts in the field of national security, including public officials and private citizens and military leaders and civilians, took part in the conference as speakers and resource experts. The report of the conference says:

In general, the program of SCUSA VI was similar to that employed in faculty level conferences, particularly the Brookings Institution's annual seminars on international affairs. The examination and discussion of the Conference subject were undertaken by the student participants themselves, working in small roundtable groups. Periodically during the [3-day] Conference, however, plenary sessions were held during which distinguished speakers assisted the conferees' deliberations by outlining for them major problems which they should

[18] "The National Security Policy of the United States," *Sixth Student Conference on United States Affairs* (West Point, N.Y.: U.S. Military Academy, 1954), p. 4.

consider. These men . . . underscored well the practical difficulties inherent in the formulation and implementation of policy.[19]

In the round-table discussions analysis of the topic led to formulation of a written report by each group:

> The final day . . . was devoted to amendment, approval, and presentation of the roundtable reports. In the morning the two tables assigned to each area of the Conference subject held a joint session, during which their committees read to them a draft of their report. Changes and additions were proposed, discussed, and compromises effected where necessary. . . . The Third Plenary Session was convened for the presentation of each of these reports.[20]

The West Point Conference is an outstanding event for a selected group of student leaders, worthy of emulation in all regions of the country.

SCUSA has, indeed, been emulated in one region, at a conference held in December 1955 at Texas Agricultural and Mechanical College, designated as SCONA I (Student Conference on National Affairs). Attended by carefully selected delegates from forty-seven colleges which included students from Canada and Mexico, financed by funds which students raised in Houston, addressed by experienced specialists in international relations, and characterized chiefly by round-table discussions leading to well-formulated reports, the conference was an impressive demonstration of informal education for able students.

Many other illustrations of special events in college life which have direct relation to education about world affairs could be cited. These vary from informal to tightly structured meetings, from recreational enterprises to highly intellectual undertakings. Some are confined to one campus; others have the stimulation, and sometimes the rivalry, of interinstitutional meetings. Experience would indicate that the events which make the greatest impact on the education of students combine recreational and intellectual interests; involve the cooperation of students, faculty,

[19] *Ibid.*, p. 5.
[20] *Ibid.*, p. 52.

and administration; involve hard effort and serious work by individual participants; and merge academic study of significant issues with some form of reasonably realistic action about the issues. Very frequently, too, those events which extend beyond the campus and involve cooperation with reputable outside agencies have added power.

Conclusion

The variety of student activities referred to in this chapter obviously constitutes only one aspect of college life. It has been emphasized that such activities as are involved in special-interest clubs, journalism, debating, and participation in student campaigns and college events can contribute to education about world affairs. To contribute effectively, they must be developed in an atmosphere of mutual interest by both students and faculty. In developing an all-college program of education about world affairs, the specialist in international relations may enhance his effectiveness by informal, out-of-class activities of this character.

—————————————————————————*CHAPTER FIVE*

Student Travel

*With the Renaissance and the revival of the classics, new values had
taken hold of man's imagination. Liberal education based on encyclo-
pedic information and the use of reason—and criticism—became the
standard for European society. In this new concept of education
travel abroad had an important function for, as Montaigne said, it
allowed young people to bring back the characteristics of those nations and their manner of living, and to rub and file our wits against
those of others.—Guy Metroux, Exchange of Persons: The Evolution
of Cross-Cultural Education.*

TRAVEL FOR educational reasons has always been important
in American life. Through the eighteenth and nineteenth centuries young and aspiring American intellectuals rounded out
their education in the cultural centers of Europe, going there
sometimes as regularly enrolled students in European universities and sometimes in the manner of Englishmen making the
"grand tour," armed with letters of introduction to leading personalities, traveling to broaden their outlooks and enrich their
minds generally rather than for purposes of specific instruction
and training. Most of the leading figures in American academic
life during the first century and a half of national existence were
European-trained or at least the beneficiaries of extended
European sojourns. The men who made modern American uni-

141

versities drew heavily upon familiarity with European universities; the evolution of the arts and sciences to which universities are devoted has long profited from exchange of ideas through exchange of persons.

Most earlier travel was personally financed, personally arranged and managed, and focused on personal interests and objectives. It was, to a major degree, limited to the economically advantaged or to the particularly adventuresome. During the twentieth century, however, marked changes have occurred in educational travel. It has been organized extensively as a group business, has touched those of economic levels for whom travel was formerly almost prohibited, has borrowed techniques from big-business "tourist industry," has become a matter of governmental concern both in terms of regulation and of aid, and has developed a new relationship to formal educational institutions and organizations. These changes, still in process, warrant close examination of the phenomena of student travel by those who are realistically concerned about informal collegiate education for world affairs.

The motives of travel for students have been markedly influenced by the international events of recent decades. To the personal interests of earlier travelers have been added many overtones of national interest, of regional welfare, of international relations. Such public interests as the development of an ill-defined but aspiring "international understanding," or the technical development of underdeveloped areas, or propagandistic activities have become involved in some student travel. The same variety of motives which brings foreign students to the United States [1] operates in varied ways to attract American students to other lands. The desire to acquire specific educational training (as to learn a language, or to study philosophy or

[1] See *The Goals of Student Exchange: An Analysis of Goals of Programs for Foreign Students* (New York: Committee on Educational Interchange Policy, January 1955).

medicine, or to learn to paint) or to further international under-standing, or to see what the rest of the world is like, or to have a good time, or to acquire the prestige of a traveler, or to make friends for the United States—all these and other motives are found among American students traveling abroad. In some cases certain of these motivations are involved in projects or programs for foreign travel, and students may share them or accept them as additions to their personal interests. At any rate, most students going abroad are now made to feel them-selves part of a movement; there is a certain self-conscious social interest, even the interest of being an "unofficial ambassador," in much of student travel today.

Contradictions and confusions among the objectives of stu-dent travelers cause considerable uncertainty and academic suspicion. Student travel merges into tourist travel and also into business travel "on mission" among organized student groups. It is technically very difficult to define student travel. Recognizing these difficulties, the data in Table 8 still evidence

TABLE 8

TOTAL NUMBER OF PASSPORTS ISSUED, 1949–53, WITH NUMBER
ISSUED TO STUDENTS AND TO PERSONS TRAVELING
FOR PURPOSE OF EDUCATION*

Year	Total Passports Issued	Stated Occupation: Student	Stated Objective of Travel: Education
1949.............	268,863	23,685	19,447
1950.............	299,665	29,546	13,837
1951.............	290,407	23,966	17,732
1952.............	395,337	34,374	28,800
1953.............	418,170	29,577	22,137

* Data furnished by Passport Office, U.S. State Department.

the importance and scope of student travel today. The number of those who list themselves as students or indicate their objective in travel as education is a surprising proportion of the total number of applicants for passports each year.

In this discussion the term "student travel" refers primarily to those American travelers who are enrolled in institutions of higher education, or who are traveling as a postcommencement culminating experience for their collegiate education. Actual arrangements and facilities for student travel will doubtless apply to more than this restricted group. Under the exigencies of booking passage student ships will often carry teachers and sometimes older tourists, for example, and many student tours will be organized for students and nonstudents together. This will more particularly be true so long as colleges and universities do not take initiative in lifting the study quality of educational tours. The questions to be dealt with in this discussion are those which concern the role of students and faculty and administration in the further systematic development of student travel in such fashion as to enhance to the fullest its intellectual and aesthetic potential for education in world outlook.

Student Travel before World War II

A major development in student travel in recent decades has been the organization of group travel projects and the development of systematic, continuing travel programs. It is still true, of course, that very many students prefer to travel individually and to let an itinerary develop as they go, but increasing numbers of students now travel in organized group "study tours," and the evidence now available seems to support such group enterprises on both financial and learning grounds. Many developments in group travel for students parallel those for general tourists so far as management and organization go. Mark Twain reported in *Innocents Abroad* an organized cultural tour for American adults in 1867, and by the end of the nineteenth century such organized and guided tours were commonplace for tourists. Travel agencies of all kinds had developed to sell their services to the itinerant. By the 1880's Brownell's Tours, the oldest such agency now in operation, were regularly taking groups of Americans, young and old, on organized tours of Europe. In later years the agency began increasingly to emphasize student tours; in 1955 it advertised its services as particularly concerned with students and serious-minded travelers under thirty.

In 1891 H. H. Powers organized in Massachusetts the Bureau of University Travel, an endowed, nonprofit organization created to conduct European tours of a collegiate quality. With its policies controlled by a Board of Trustees consisting largely of university professors who believed that "travel under inspirational leadership is one of the highest forms of education," and with many of its tours led by outstanding scholarly experts, the bureau very early assumed the character of an important extracurricular activity in which many academic people and institutions were interested. In some respects both the bureau and Brownell's Tours were travel equivalents of the Chautauqua movement. During the years since 1950 the bureau has organized an American College Council for Summer Study Abroad, through which some two-score colleges and universities share in offering traveling courses dealing with the history, art, literature, languages, and international relations of European countries.

Many other agencies were organized and operated briefly to facilitate organized student travel in the early years of the present century, but major impetus to student travel came in the years following World War I and again after the end of World War II. During the years since 1919 there have been many organized student tours under a wide variety of auspices, and interest in student travel on the part of youth-serving agencies and organizations has grown markedly. By the mid-1950's it is estimated that at least 20,000 American students are abroad each summer and an additional 30,000 for year-round study or research abroad. A small but significant number of these students are out of the country "on mission" for various youth groups, conducting the international relations of organized students themselves. A considerable number are abroad annually for systematic study in the universities and institutes and laboratories and studios of other nations. The great majority travel for general educational purposes, either as individuals or in organized study tour groups. Student missions vary greatly as to time involved; regularly enrolled students abroad spend ordinarily more than a year away from home; study tours and individual summer trips, a poor man's equivalent of the European "grand tour," usually last for eight or ten weeks. The effect of a foreign sojourn naturally varies among students—the variation due both to the psychological character of the participant and to the quality of the travel experience—but, in general, travel is a major influence in determining attitudes and in providing background information. In the survey of sources of college seniors' outlook on world affairs which was reported in chapter 3, seniors who had traveled rated travel as the most significant factor in shaping their outlook.

A number of organizations which sponsor student travel have their origin in the decade and a half following World War I. Among these the Experiment in International Living has an outstanding record.[2] Organized in the early 1930's by Donald Watt, it emphasizes the importance of friendly, informal relations for the young traveler in the host country. The Experiment arranges for groups which it sponsors to live in homes abroad, becoming for a few weeks members of families in a selected foreign community. The visitors associate with young people of their own age, take hiking and bicycling and boating

[2] See "An Introduction to the Experiment in International Living; Its History, Method, Scope, and Program" (Mimeographed; 1st ed.; Putney, Vermont, 1955).

trips with them, and as nearly as possible live the life of the country visited. In its forty years of existence the Experiment has organized foreign living experience for more than four thousand American students. With 24 Experimenters in 1932, it had grown to 527 in 1955. For these students the Experiment headquarters at Putney, Vermont, are a continuing channel for international contacts. The Experiment has developed relations with a number of colleges, notably Colgate, by which students going on Experiment trips may concentrate on learning a language and subsequently receive academic credit based on progress and accomplishment. In recent years the Experiment has conducted research studies on the methods and effects of interchange of persons and has brought numbers of foreign students for visits in American homes. It is an educational agency of established reputation, popular and influential on many campuses.

Another travel organization dating from the early 1930's is SITA, the Students' International Travel Association. It began as a series of bicycling trips abroad, organized inexpensively and focusing on simple living and friendly contacts away from the tourist centers. It early emphasized language study and direct contact with organized youth groups in the countries visited. Founded and developed by Jack and Helen Dengler, it has expanded widely; some twelve thousand students and teachers have participated in SITA study tours since 1934. By 1955 it was offering study tours carrying credit in a variety of subject fields in cooperation with a group of colleges and universities located in North and South America, Europe, and Hawaii. Organized and managed as a business corporation, it nevertheless focuses attention on worthy educational objectives.

Founded in Europe in 1910, the International Youth Hostel Federation now includes national organizations in twenty-nine countries; the American Youth Hostel (AYH) became a member of the federation in 1934. Serving every age group, the hostels provide inexpensive and simple, often austere, accommodations for travelers engaging in hiking or bicycling, canoeing, or horse-back trips. Hostels are open to members who live up to the rules of the association; hostelers travel individually or in small groups. Youth hostels are entirely extracurricular, but the in-expensiveness and simplicity of AYH tours in other countries appeal to many students on American campuses.

Another educational travel development of the 1930's, rooted entirely in the curriculum itself, is the Junior Year Abroad program. Under the program qualified American students may spend their junior year abroad, in Paris or Geneva for example, taking courses in a foreign university under the immediate guidance and supervision of a tutor representing an American college or university which grants academic credit for work well done. Originating in a desire to provide superior language instruction for students, the various junior year abroad programs now enroll students in a variety of fields of study. Yale sends a group which includes selected students from various American universities to France each year. Smith sends students both to Paris and Geneva. Hollins College is experimenting with a group resident abroad for the second semester of the sophomore and the first semester of the junior years. Sweet Briar College sends a group widely drawn from the United States to France each year. The University of Maryland provides a similar ar-rangement of foreign study under resident tutorial supervision for graduate students.

There is little doubt that a junior year abroad is a highly significant experience for the limited number who participate in it. Returning students attest to its popularity and value. In some cases there are difficulties of adjustment during the senior year arising not from study abroad but simply from absence from the campus during a critical part of the collegiate quadren-nium, but these difficulties fade before the positive merits of the foreign sojourn. For economic reasons, the Junior Year Abroad program can affect only a few students, but even so the program does not now seem to be sponsored and supported on as many campuses as its merit warrants.

The four travel programs just listed represent widely varied approaches to a field which developed rapidly during the 1920's and 1930's, even during the depression years. These four are only a few of many enterprises, among which church-related programs should be noted. Study tours by the Catholic student groups, Pax Romana and the Newman Clubs, as well as the organizational activities and contacts of such international associations, flourished on American campuses. The American Friends Service Committee's program gave substantial numbers of deeply motivated students experience in service abroad, as in its work-camp projects and in the study of international questions through its student summer seminars. The Unitarian and Universalist Service Committees, the Brethren Service Commission, the World Council of Churches, the United Student Christian Councils, and the National Student Councils of the Young Men's and Young Women's Christian Associations developed travel programs involving work camps, summer study, special institutes, and service opportunities abroad. World War II inevitably suspended many of the travel activities which had earlier developed or shifted them temporarily into Latin-American and domestic tours, but after the war interest in such enterprises was stronger than ever before.

Student Travel since 1945

General interest in world affairs and the varied cultures of the world reached a new peak in the United States after World War II, and this interest was reflected in all phases of college life. Increased numbers of students began to feel that seeing a foreign country was a part of being educated. The presence of many widely traveled veterans on campus doubtless contributed to the desire for travel. So too did curricular developments which stressed cultural differences and contacts, and which brought to students' attention earlier neglected areas of the world. Extraordinary changes in facilities of transportation, particularly in aviation, helped fire the travel imagination of students. And above all else the continuing involvement of the United States in world affairs and the unrest and insecurity arising from the cold war impelled students to "see the world" as they had never done before.

The great impetus for student travel between 1945 and 1955 came not from off-campus agencies, but from the campuses themselves. While many of the older travel organizations developed new programs to meet the new interests and opportunities, student organizations and individual professors took increased initiative in organizing tours of every conceivable description. Many of the plans which were developed proved feasible and worth while and have been continued. But other of the attempts, flamboyantly advertised in their early stages, were fortunately abortive. A good many tours promoted by the inexperienced or the evangelistic or the ambitious-to-travel which managed to get off the ground, so to speak, failed to achieve worthy educational results. Some of them were wrecked in mid-passage, leaving students stranded in Europe until extra financial help could reach them. Numbers of colleges were embarrassed and their administrators embittered against student travel by the extravagant claims of naïve students or professors who were travel-minded. In a few cases there was actual chicanery in the collection and use of student travel funds; more frequently there was poor business management. A number of tours abroad proved to be embarrassing to the United States by making unwarranted demands on our own Embassies and on perplexed officials of other countries.

In spite of all these fumblings, false starts, and ludicrous and unwarranted enterprises, the full story of student travel in the postwar decade is an encouraging one. When the balance sheet is examined, the record of student travel abroad is extremely good, both in terms of its education of students and in terms of the development of better understanding between visitors and visited. Certain of the outstandingly successful enterprises of the decade may illustrate this point.[3]

One of the better and continuing enterprises, known as SPAN —Student Project for Amity among Nations—developed just after World War II at the University of Minnesota. There a group of students sought specifically to develop travel projects worthy of academic status and contributory to long-range international understanding. The student group secured the active cooperation of a number of faculty members and the blessings of the administration for an enterprise which now involves most of the institutions of higher education in Minnesota and annually sends from thirty to fifty carefully prepared students abroad for systematic, organized group travel, observation, and study.

An organization of students and faculty advisers manages the SPAN program. Each year the group decides what countries will be visited by SPAN students during the following summer and selects a faculty leader for each team of eight or ten students. Applications are received from students for admission to the selected tours, and after tryout tests, a student-faculty

[3] Each year the Institute of International Education presents a listing of foreign summer schools open to students from the United States. *Summer Study Abroad 1955* includes only those courses which are sponsored by foreign educational institutions. Information on courses arranged by U.S. educational and travel groups, as well as group tours which may or may not include a period of foreign study, is given in *Work, Study, Travel Abroad,* published by the National Student Association, 48 West 48th St., New York 19 (price, 50 cents). International service projects, including work camps, are to be found in *Invest Your Summer,* published by the Commission on Youth Service Projects, 79 East Adams St., Chicago 3, Ill. (price, 7 cents). Short study tours arranged by national groups and youth center activities are listed in *Study Abroad, Vacation Study Supplement,* published by UNESCO and available through the Columbia University Press, 2960 Broadway, New York 27 (price, 50 cents). Students interested in opportunities for study, work projects, study and vacation tours in Latin America should consult *Summer Study in Latin America,* published by the Pan American Union, Washington 6, D.C. (price, 10 cents).

committee carefully selects the most worthy candidates. When selected on a preliminary basis, these students begin a year's careful preparation for the trip. They study the language and the history and the present circumstances of the country to be visited. Each participating student selects a topic for his personal study "in the field"—an analysis of a phase of British politics, a series of interviews with leaders of the existentialist movement, analysis of the Secretariat of the International Labor Organization, for example—and undertakes background preparation for his field study of the topic.

In the meantime, the SPAN organization raises funds for the enterprise by solicitation throughout the state, although each student traveler is expected to pay part of his own way. The organization, too, arranges the details of travel and handles administrative matters. In this work the alumni of SPAN are deeply involved, for each participant pledges a portion of his time to the work of the organization after his return.

The SPAN summer abroad is spent in inexpensive travel and in field study on the selected topics under the immediate supervision of a Minnesota faculty member. Each student completes, soon after his return to Minnesota, a paper on his chosen topic. Submitted to the faculty of one of the sponsoring institutions, this paper, plus the instructor's report on the student, becomes the basis for granting academic credit. And for the academic year following his return the student not only gives a proportion of his time to the "office work" of organizing the next year's trip but also is obligated to speak on his experiences and observations abroad to campus groups and to adult civic and religious groups throughout the state. The decade of development through which the SPAN enterprise has now gone has made it a significant educational undertaking, has given it real prestige on its sponsoring campuses, and has illustrated the effectiveness of student-faculty cooperation in the interest of an informal educational effort. No better illustration of the effective integration of curriculum and extracurriculum could be found.

A project launched by the student group at Harvard in 1947 has involved only a minimum of trans-Atlantic travel but has developed into a major educational enterprise affecting European-American relations. A group of Harvard students, with the cooperation of a few professors but without sponsorship from the university, organized the Salzburg Seminar, center for study of the United States by young Europeans. The students secured the use of a castle in Austria, selected a staff of American professors for a summer seminar, selected 100 able young scholars from all over Europe, and raised funds to assemble the group at Salzburg and maintain them for a summer. A small number of American advanced students attended the seminar in the capacity of faculty assistants. Founded "on a shoestring" and with the determined energy of students, the seminar received later financial support from foundations, was organized on a year-round basis, and now has an established reputation throughout Europe as a center for American studies.

A quite different enterprise was organized and operated for three years (1950-53) by the Association of International Relations Clubs. The association developed a plan of study-touring which involved: (1) systematic orientation of a travel group on shipboard bound for Europe; (2) attendance for six weeks at special seminars on national cultures and international relations held in Great Britain, France, and Switzerland; (3) carefully arranged contacts with organized groups of citizens in the countries visited; and (4) a three-week period in which tour participants wandered "on their own" in European areas of their choice. The combination of systematic institutes and individual time for tourism seemed effective in increasing participants' understanding of the areas visited.

One of the AIRC tours was accompanied by two trained psychologists who conducted one of the few analyses of study tours which have been made. Reporting on this study,[4] Dr. Hilda Taba emphasized the complexities of intercultural contacts and communications, pointed out that the psychological balance and maturity of the traveler had very much to do with his reactions to other cultures and to travel experiences, suggested that some such coordinating and interpreting experiences as the AIRC institutes added measurably to travelers' understanding of their observations, and pointed out that travel is often more influential on one's assessment of his own culture than of an outside culture. While her study supports the importance of student study tours, it also indicates the desirability of much more extensive and penetrating analysis of the ways and means by which such tours may be made increasingly effective. In this area lies fruitful research for both the anthropologist-sociologist-psychologist and the educator.

Another type of student enterprise involving travel may be illustrated by Project PIC—Project Pakistan, India, Ceylon—at the University of California at Berkeley. On the West Coast particularly, but also on campuses throughout the country, interest in Asia has been increasing rapidly, as evidenced in both curriculum and extracurriculum developments. In February 1953 a group of about one hundred students on the Berkeley campus met informally to discuss the situation in Asia and the need for increased understanding between Asians and Americans. Out of their discussion grew plans for a study tour in Pakistan, India, and Ceylon.

With the belief that there is no substitute for person-to-person contact, the members of Project PIC established as their immediate goal the sending of a group of American students from the University of California to Southern Asia to meet and speak with the students and leaders of these three new democracies. It was their hope that they might contribute something to improve international relations

[4] Hilda Taba, *Cultural Attitudes and International Understanding: An Evaluation of an International Study Tour* (New York: Institute of International Education, June 1953).

and human understanding by teaching something about the United States, and by learning how they could initiate and advise private American efforts to aid the peoples of the subcontinent. In an effort to better understand the problems of Asia, an ambitious program of seminars was begun. The members of the Project met for five-hour sessions every Friday evening. They presented reports; they held discussions; they enlisted the assistance of experts in many fields. They studied the history, geography, institutions, customs, religions, art and music of Pakistan, India, and Ceylon. . . .

Soon the group recognized the advantage of decreasing its size in order to better prepare itself for the projected task. In open meetings it chose a selection committee composed of University officials and community leaders and submitted to this committee the criteria for selection. Each student then underwent a personal interview and a number of other evaluation procedures. From this large group of students, twenty-five were selected to carry on the Project.[5]

Needing funds to finance the project, students turned their attention to fund-raising even while continuing their background studies. By strenuous efforts, and with the aid of university authorities, they succeeded in securing the $30,000 required for the venture. By further selection the tour group was reduced to twelve—six men and six women—aged nineteen to twenty-three, and majoring in political science, English, social welfare, pharmacy, agriculture, and art. This smaller group spent ten weeks in Southern Asia during the summer of 1953, in a well-arranged tour from which the students gained maximum benefit. The interest they aroused continues as a force in college life at the University of California. Project PIC continues as an active force on the Berkeley campus, not only for travel but also for aid and counsel to students from the three Asiatic countries involved, and for the conduct of campaigns in aid of educational enterprises in these countries.

A somewhat similar enterprise, known as Project India, was carried on at the University of California at Los Angeles in 1952 and 1953. Organized under the sponsorship of the Uni-

[5] *Project Pakistan, India, Ceylon: A Report on a Student Effort for International Understanding* (Berkeley: PIC, Associated Students, University of California), p. 1.

versity Religious Conference, a group of students prepared themselves with great care and sensitivity for a visit to India. Their chief concern was to meet with Indian students, to discuss possibilities of student participation in college government, and to determine and appraise student-led, social-welfare projects in India on which American aid might be particularly helpful. The group of a dozen students which visited India in 1953 was divided into two teams on each of which was "one person with some background in art, one in science, one in politics or inter-national relations, one in education." [6] Moreover, the members were chosen as "a good cross-section of the average American student community. There was a good inter-faith and inter-racial mixture and the group was about evenly divided between those students who might be called introverts and extroverts." The group was selected and organized not so much on a study basis as on the basis of a mission sent to India to consult on matters of mutual concern. Following the return of the groups in both 1952 and 1953 substantial funds were raised on the Los Angeles campus in aid of student enterprises in India. Members of the India tour spoke widely before groups throughout south-ern California, contributing the honoraria received for their talks to the selected enterprises in India. A letter from the Executive Secretary of the University Religious Conference, who was instrumental in organizing Project India, reports that:

On our return from Project India 1952 the Student Council voted that the proceeds of the Fall Charity Drive that year would be given to Indian groups in which the students composing the Project had become interested. Some $2,000 was sent either in cash or edu-cational material, and there was great interest on the campus. The Project group spoke to every living group, to the library association, etc. After the return of the Project 1953 there was even greater interest, stimulated a good deal by attacks on the whole idea by the college newspaper. The drive this year netted some $3,000, and

---

[6] Adeline C. Guenther, "Report on Project India: 1955" (Mimeographed; Los Angeles: University of California at Los Angeles, 1955), p. 2.

there was in addition a report to the whole campus, made at an assembly for which classes were dismissed. . . .

Another type of summer travel has been developed by the Western College for Women at Oxford, Ohio. Emphasis is placed on international relations in the entire organization and curriculum of the college. Representatives of foreign cultures are regularly on the faculty as permanent appointees or visiting professors. Approximately 12 percent of the women enrolled in the college come from outside the United States. Each year there is emphasis throughout the college on one world area; a four-year cycle is followed in the study of Latin America, the Far East, the Near East, and Europe. Special visiting lecturers, exhibits, film showings, and courses focus attention on the area during the chosen period. The area emphasis is climaxed by a summer tour, arranged for such students and faculty as are able to go, with particular appeal to students who have just completed the junior year. In the summer of 1955, for example, a party of thirty-two people, including the college president and ten members of the faculty, spent July on a tour of Peru, Chile, Argentina, Brazil, and Venezuela. Detailed study programs in each of the countries had been set up in cooperation with committees made up of alumnae of the college. Emphasis was placed on three interests—the culture of the country visited, the impact of the United States technically and culturally on the country, and the educational practices and theories of the country. No college credit is given for the tour; it is regarded as an enrichment of the college curriculum and is given high prestige by students and faculty alike.[7] The program of the succeeding academic year for those who have taken the tour is arranged to utilize and build on their field experience. The fact that members of the faculty and representatives of the student body tour together in a study-and-recreation enterprise has further merit

[7] See Herrick B. Young, "No Academic Credit for Travel Abroad," *School and Society*, May 28, 1955, pp. 168–69.

in heightening the sense of community in the college throughout the academic year.

The number of American universities which, by either student or faculty initiative or both, sponsor or recognize officially study tours outside the United States is rapidly increasing. Beaver College in Pennsylvania has long sent students abroad on systematic study tours each summer. Boston University operates regularly high-level, low-cost educational tours. In 1953 the State College of Washington sponsored a European tour for the study of Renaissance art and a tour for the study of Mexican history and culture. A statement from Howard Lee Nostrand in 1952 on "Pacific Northwest Colleges and World Affairs" [8] reports a field class in European geography for students at Oregon College of Education, a summer session in Sweden sponsored by the College of Puget Sound, a Willamette study tour in France, and University of Washington tours in France, Germany, and Spain. Since 1953 Miami University has sponsored each summer a Miami University Abroad. These are but a few illustrations of a widespread academic interest in student travel.

The National Student Association became a leading agency in the field of student travel after its organization in 1948. It organized summer tours, often in cooperation with the student associations of other countries; most of its tours were purely recreational, while others were more study-oriented in character. In its earlier years, operated by inexperienced students who were belligerent toward "competitors," some of the NSA tours seemed hampered by overoptimistic management. Although its growth had not been without periods of crisis, the association could report by 1955 that "USNSA's Travel Department has grown into a self-sustaining, nonprofit organization benefiting hundreds of American students every year." In 1955, in addition to sight-

[8] Nostrand, "Pacific Northwest Colleges and World Affairs," *Universities and World Affairs*, Document No. 10 (Mimeographed; New York: Carnegie Endowment for International Peace, 1952).

seeing tours in most European countries, it offered tours
involving contacts with persons and places in the fields of
journalism, music, painting and sculpture, sociology, sports,
engineering, medicine and public health, business and commerce.
While most of these tours were substantial, they did not embody
clear-cut academic features or new methods of combining curriculum and extracurriculum. Perhaps the outstanding tour
groups arranged by NSA thus far have been those designed for
campus leaders in student government, providing opportunity
for meeting with leaders of student associations in other countries and for the discussion of international student relations.
In addition to such summer tours the missions sent to all parts
of the world by USNSA for the purpose of working with student
associations elsewhere on problems of mutual concern provided
unusually significant travel experience for a limited number of
able young men and women.

In addition to the varied study tours which have been developed by American organizations and institutions for student
travelers, a growing number of summer schools and institutes
organized in other countries appeal to many United States students and faculty members. Most European and some Latin-
American countries now offer summer programs emphasizing
language or study of the culture of the country concerned. Some
of these programs are six-week summer schools; others are ten-
day or two-week institutes. For illustration, in 1955, the University of Innsbruck offered four sessions of three weeks each on
German language and literature; the International People's College at Elsinore scheduled three two-week sessions on Modern
Denmark; France offered no less than twenty-eight summer
programs; Oxford developed a six-week program on Politics and
Literature of the Twentieth Century. Opportunities for summer
study abroad are increasing in a wide variety of academic fields.
Such study possibilities as these attract each year several hundred Americans, students and older people alike.

Council on Student Travel

A decade after the end of World War II student travel had reached a new peak for the United States. In 1955 the "professional" tour groups specializing in student travel—such groups as Brownell's Tours, the Bureau of University Travel, the Experiment in International Living, American Youth Hostels, divers church-related groups, the Student International Travel Association, the National Student Association—arranged summer trips, more or less educational in character, for more than ten thousand American students, and an equal number of students traveled as individuals. For the organized tours, the most difficult problems of transportation, organization, and orientation which had baffled travel programs in the late 1940's were no longer so baffling. The overambitious and underexperienced organizers of student travel had fallen by the wayside. With the problems somewhat eased, and with rising academic interest in travel, program organizers were able to turn their attention increasingly to qualitative improvements.

One of the agencies responsible for the general improvement of standards of student travel is the Council on Student Travel. The council was organized in 1947 when the rising interest in student travel seemed thwarted by a lack of ship space. A number of interested organizations formed the council, which negotiated with the United States Maritime Commission to secure the use of troop transports for operation by United States Lines. Two converted troopships were put in operation, "chartered at the request of the Department of State for the express purpose of transporting students and cultural groups across to Europe and back." [9] The council not only negotiated the use of the ships but also organized extensive orientation programs for students using the ships. The council's orientation services

[9] See Philip E. Jacob, "Floating Seminars, 1947: Training for International Understanding," *Social Education*, January 1948, pp. 23–27.

were employed by the organized student tours; shipboard instruction in language, cultural contrasts, current affairs, and international relations while en route across the Atlantic proved so successful, in fact, that by 1955 the council was under contract to provide such programs for regular tourists on a number of commercial trans-Atlantic lines.

Organized and operated initially on an *ad hoc* basis, the council gradually developed into a permanent organization with a year-round staff and services. By 1950 the government no longer made transports available for student travel, and in 1951 the council began to charter ships, assuming the management of shipping arrangements and the financial responsibilities involved. By 1955 the council contracted for space on eight ships capable of caring for 7,125 student passages and entered into long-term contracts for shipping space which would further tend to stabilize the problem of student shipping. There is now available considerable space for low-cost student travel, efficiently administered by the permanent staff of the council. The 38 organizations which are members of the council and its half-dozen associate members receive regular allotments of ship space each year, but other student groups and qualified individuals are also served. During the eight years of the council's existence it has provided space for almost 25,000 traveling students; in 1954 it served approximately 5,000 American students from 329 colleges and universities.

Organized to meet the problem of shipping space, the council has from its inception also assumed responsibility for shipboard orientation programs; as has been indicated, this responsibility has been well discharged. The council also serves as an information center and clearinghouse, handling large numbers of inquiries and maintaining a tour-referral service. It convenes an annual mid-winter Conference on Student Travel which provides a forum for exchange of ideas and at which travel agencies, commercial and noncommercial, consult with student and faculty tour leaders and representatives of shipping lines. Its annual conference is perhaps the chief meeting each year for persons concerned with this field and has become increasingly professional in character.

In many respects the council serves the same accrediting function in the student travel field that the various professional accrediting associations serve in American academic fields. Its by-laws provide strict rules for its members:

To be eligible for active membership in the Council, an organization or institution must be a bona fide non-profit educational, civic, or religious organization and must conduct some type of international educational travel program or render some service to organizations conducting such programs. It must be governed by a qualified and responsible Board of Directors, and must have demonstrated for a period of three years its educational competence and financial responsibility.

Associate membership in the council is restricted to commercial organizations which maintain high educational standards and are competently managed. Periodic review of the standards and programs of member organizations and applicants for membership is conducted to ensure that eligibility requirements are maintained. The strict adherence of the council to qualitative operations has served to eliminate a number of unreliable programs; at the same time the council staff is in continual consultative service to legitimate and worthy study tour enterprises in process of development on a wide variety of campuses. The three-year operation requirement for membership is a probationary period during which council advice is available. The council raises standards, too, by a program of field studies in student travel, and by the publication of brochures of value to tour leaders and individual travelers.[10]

[10] See, for example, the published *Reports* on the annual Conferences on Student Travel, as well as *Travelers' Information: A Bibliography of Educational Material for the Orientation of Travelers* (April 1955), which may be secured from the Council on Student Travel, 179 Broadway, New York 7, N.Y.

Problems and Issues

There are, of course, many problems and issues in the field of organized student travel; these are its inevitable growing pains. Research is needed on the relative merits of study tour programs, on the relation of psychological characteristics of the traveler to the effects of travel on him, on the personal adjustments and outlooks which are amenable to orientation programs, on the relation of cultural distance to mutual understanding. This research has hardly yet begun, but the potential contribution of travel to education in world relations makes the research area most promising. [11]

A basic factor in determining the educational value of travel is, for students, its relationship to the college and university. If the educational institution takes no responsibility for student travel, the travel is likely to be relatively touristic; if the institution is involved in planning and management, there is relative emphasis on the study side of a study tour. In cases where students and faculty work together on a plan which is rooted in the work of the college or university, the best travel programs are developed, and the best educative results seem to be secured. The institutions of higher education which are now pioneering in travel programs, often in close collaboration with established and experienced travel agencies, are opening new paths particularly appropriate to the conditions of the contemporary world.

Questions of academic credit for study-travel arise repeatedly to irritate both tour managers and college administrators as well as traveling students. Until more research has been completed on the nature and effectiveness of study tours, no general answer can be found to the problem of credit. Certainly academic credit should not be given for inferior work or for idle travel, but such

[11] See Cora Du Bois, *Foreign Students and Higher Education in the United States* (Washington: American Council on Education, 1956).

arrangements as have been developed in the Junior Year Abroad and in Minnesota's SPAN program seem entirely defensible as warranting academic recognition. It would seem appropriate, too, for universities to analyze carefully the relation of travel to particular degree programs. For advanced degrees in certain fields, perhaps in language or area studies or aspects of geography, foreign travel may well become requisite. Carefully supervised travel may be a worthy element in honors programs for the baccalaureate. Institutions, particularly those on the quarter system, may do well to explore the possibilities of off-season travel for students within the customary academic year. Certainly in a world as small as ours has become and for the education of men and women who cannot escape international responsibilities, extensive experimentation with academically planned travel is desirable.

Observing student travel as a whole, one is impressed with the extent to which it is trans-Atlantic travel. Europe receives a very high proportion of the American students who travel; the organized programs and the physical facilities for European travel are better developed than for travel into other areas. Yet, as the examples of travel projects given in this chapter indicate, there is widespread interest in Asia, and to a less extent, interest in Africa and Latin America, among American students. A number of student groups have successfully developed Asian travel enterprises; the World University Service is particularly interested in encouraging travel in Asia. Within time the material problems of cost, transportation, and time may be solved, but the study-tour methods and policies which are most appropriate for travel in Europe may not be most suitable for travel in Asia. Cultural distance as a factor in contacts between American and Asian students warrants extremely careful study. Aware of these and similar problems, organizations interested in student travel to Asia have begun systematically to explore them. In December 1954 sixty-seven persons representing twenty-four

American organizations met in Putney, Vermont, under the auspices of the Experiment in International Living to explore the problems and to pool their experience.[12] Considerable expansion in student travel to Asia and other relatively unvisited areas seems likely for the immediate future.

Conclusion

Organized student travel projects such as those described illustrate admirably a cocurricular approach to collegiate education about world affairs. Developments in this field in recent decades, and particularly since 1945, afford evidence that student travel can be exciting and challenging without being merely touristic recreation, and that it can be serious and responsible without being dull. It presents problems, but these are not insurmountable. The resources exist for solving material transportation problems, although these problems take on new dimensions as student interests shift toward Asia and Latin America and Africa. The problems of preparation for travel have been solved with academic distinction by such programs as SPAN, and the development of shipboard orientation programs, even for tourists, is a notable recent advance. A number of institutions have experimented with academic credit for responsible travel, and the results warrant further experimentation in this field. The closer coordination of formal instruction with field study abroad would seem to be meritorious as well as feasible in a number of academic fields.

[12] See "Report of the Conference on North American Youth Activities in Asia, Africa and the Middle East" (Mimeographed; Putney, Vermont: Experiment in International Living, 1954).

CHAPTER SIX

Organizing College Life

Political education is not merely a matter of coming to understand a tradition, it is learning how to participate in a conversation; it is at once initiation into an inheritance in which we have a life interest, and the exploration of its intimations. There will always remain something of a mystery about how a tradition of political behavior is learned, and perhaps the only certainty is that there is no point at which learning it can properly be said to begin. The politics of a community are not less individual (and not more so) than its language, and they are learned and practiced in the same manner.—Michael Oakeshott, Political Education.

THE OPENING PAGES of this volume suggested that "in the actuality of college living its divers chords and melodies are too rarely orchestrated." In succeeding pages a good many chords and melodies and individual notes have been described as items in the life of a college community. Some have been praised and some doubted, but the general effect thus far has been to present college life in terms of a wide and varied range of activities. All these chords and melodies do not necessarily make a symphony. The problems of interrelationship and coordination and balance among the items of campus living must be solved if the collegiate way of life is to contribute adequately to the education of its citizens. The traditional functions of the college and university have a major stake in this coordination.

166

Without coordination, balance, and structure campus life may not only scatter the energies of youth but may also add to confusion of values and to internal conflicts and tensions. At the same time it is easily possible to overorganize campus affairs to the point where all pleasure and most meaning are squeezed out of them. No such extreme is here envisaged; no such extreme is necessary for harmoniously and creatively orchestrating college life. Obviously there must be flexibility, variety, room for initiative and development. What is here proposed is the kind of civic arrangement and orderliness which characterizes any good community. A reasonable orderliness avoids duplication of clubs and events and activities; it keeps a calendar balanced; it contributes to all phases of education, including informal education about world affairs. The proposals of this volume were, in a sense, stated by a professor of English writing in the *Journal of Higher Education*. Commenting on campus life, he suggests:

. . . that we provide intellectual interests and aesthetic satisfactions on the campus through the medium of the extra-curriculum . . . concerted faculty action to lift student activities from vicious vapidity . . . that we establish the campus community as a pattern of intellectual and aesthetic activity, a pattern of living which students will recognize and value . . . which they will take with them when they leave . . . as educated persons.[1]

Both students and faculties have been much concerned in recent years about the organizing of campus life, making their concern manifest in a good many proposals and developments in all types of colleges and universities. Systems of student government—or, more appropriately, of student participation in college government—have developed at the same time that the offices of deans of students have come into existence and that committees of faculty and trustees have been created to deal with college life. In this chapter student participation in indi-

[1] Martin Staples Shockley, "The Extra-Curriculum," *Journal of Higher Education*, December 1953, p. 459.

vidual campus government, the work of the National Student Association, and all-university policies and programs for developing college life by both students and faculty will be examined, with particular reference to the organization of campus activities dealing with education in international matters.

Student Participation in College Government

The great variety of student clubs and activities which characterize most campuses is, with varying degrees of success, brought into a measure of symmetry and coordination by the machinery of student participation in government. Student government appeared in American colleges during Revolutionary War years, at William and Mary in 1779. A simple arrangement was established by which a student-elected committee handled routine disciplinary problems and minor improvement projects. When Oberlin was founded in 1833,

there was provision for student participation and cooperation in institutional management. . . . These students were the "first ancestors of [modern style] student government in higher education." [2]

By the 1920's there was some form of all-student association on almost every campus. There was much talk of student government as an apprenticeship in democracy. In the newer, experimental institutions founded during and after the 1920's, steps were usually taken to give students a fair voice in the management of the college community.

Student government, though often modeled arbitrarily after the federal example, displayed an infinite variety of forms. In some instances, the power of student government was virtually absolute within a definitely restricted area; in other places the student government developed with a little power over a lot of

[2] Frances E. Falvey, *Student Participation in College Administration* (New York: Bureau of Publications, Teachers College, Columbia University, 1952), p. 41.

things. It was ordinarily concerned with exclusively extra-curricular enterprises and with disciplinary functions. In some places student government was only a mask for faculty domination or administrator control; the complaint is still heard on many campuses that leaders in student government are the subservient instruments of administration. In many places schemes of student government fell as victims of immature student politics. However, from the welter of experimentation with forms and functions of student government there emerged, as the decades of the twentieth century passed, relatively mature and responsible patterns and structures contributing to the integration of campus life. The functions of student government as they have come to be viewed in this decade have been well formulated by Brother Louis of St. Mary's College in Minnesota. Student government, as he sees it, should:

1. Have the responsibility for the operation and control of all student organizations of the college campus.
2. Have the responsibility for promoting, organizing, and directing what might be termed "all-college" functions and programs. . . .
3. Have a definite responsibility for the formation of policies concerning all student life and student activities. . . .
4. Should provide the means for achieving mutual understanding and close cooperation between students, faculty, and administration.[3]

It is not the purpose of this study to analyze in general terms the function and structure of student governing associations or to appraise their general values and weaknesses. But to indicate the scope of student government in a modern university and at the same time to outline its relationship to education about world affairs, the organization of the Associated Students of Stanford University may be described.

The *Stanford Handbook* for 1954 informs new students that for over fifty years the center of student government at Stanford

[3] Brother Louis, "The Role of Student Government in the Student Personnel Program," *Educational and Psychological Measurement*, Autumn 1950, pp. 570–71.

University has been an Executive Committee (Excom) elected by the entire student body.

The students have had the power to legislate, administer, and judge student affairs by themselves. . . . The members of Excom are elected fall and spring in a staggered system, so that sound leadership will be provided by having experienced members at all times. Representation is by a combined class and living group basis. Each undergraduate class has its own representative, and the graduates have two members. There are representatives from each of the [seven] living groups. . . . Excom meets every Wednesday night in open session. Here members of the student body are given the opportunity to air their problems and watch their government in action.

The ASSU President is the directing force in all student activities. . . . He is the students' official spokesman at outside conferences and serves as a representative of the ASSU on the Union Board of Governors, the Stanford Athletic Board.

The Vice-President, usually a coed, directs and coordinates all the campus social affairs. She keeps the ASSU Social Calendar, which includes every on- or off-campus social function, up-to-date, and also tries to keep it filled with enough activities consistently throughout the year.

. . . .

The Constitution and By-laws of the ASSU as administered by Excom are the basis of all student government. . . . All ASSU officers have their offices at the Union with regular hours for appointments with interested students.[4]

The Associated Students of Stanford University operate through a variety of councils, committees, and boards in addition to its central authority, the Executive Committee. In subordinate relation to it are Men's and Women's Councils; a group of juniors and seniors known as Cardinals, which promotes college spirit; a society which cultivates off-campus relations; a Publications Board; a Public Relations Board; a Social Coordinating Board; and a Student Health Committee.

Two student agencies at Stanford organized under the Executive Committee have direct relationship to international interests

---

[4] Associated Students and Stanford University, *The Stanford Handbook: 1954–1955*, Vol. 60, pp. 20–21.

—the Foreign Scholarship Committee and the students' Institute of International Relations. The Foreign Scholarship Committee, with high social prestige on the campus, raises necessary funds for a group of foreign-student scholarships, selects the students to be awarded the scholarships, makes arrangements for room and board for foreign students in the fraternities and women's residences, and aids in orienting foreign students into the life of the university.

The Institute of International Relations, which theoretically embraces all Stanford students in its membership and actually involves several hundred students annually in its program, is relatively unique among student groups. Under student leadership and management it organizes two large conferences each year—a Western College Conference on American Foreign Policy and a week-end UNESCO Conference for high school representatives from the state. It maintains on the campus a United Nations Education Center which distributes films and literature on international subjects and publishes monthly bulletins on the United Nations for high schools and colleges throughout northern California. Its International Club is a social organization to bring foreign and American students together. The institute conducts campaigns "through solicitation, auctions, dances, and novelty stunts" by which some $10,000 are raised yearly for international relief work. It collects and distributes information on work, study, and travel abroad for students, and occasionally organizes a student overseas tour. It maintains an affiliation relationship with Keio University in Japan and with the Free University of Berlin.

To the institute's activities many students who are particularly but not necessarily professionally interested in world affairs give many hours of service. Under certain conditions limited academic credit is given for some of its work; it cooperates closely with faculty specialists in international relations and with such off-campus groups as the Student World Affairs Council of

Northern California, the Collegiate Council for the United Nations, the World University Service, and the Association of International Relations Clubs. A special bulletin describing the institute summarizes its function by saying:

The Institute of International Relations is not a club, but a nonpartisan, non-profit, democratic, student-run organization. It is an official part of the student government and is subject to the authority of the Executive Committee of the Associated Students of Stanford University. The primary function of the Institute is outlined in Article IV, Section 62, of the ASSU By-laws: "The Institute shall have the responsibility for the conduct of the foreign affairs of the Associated Students and the coordination, administration, and regulation of all international activities." From this it can be seen that the IIR is the working nerve center of all the student body's international activities. Its primary purpose is to contribute to peace and security through those means most available to university students, namely, *education* and *service*.[5]

It is unnecessary to observe that the Stanford machinery of student participation in government, including its Institute of International Relations, does not always work perfectly. It is as subject to human failings, rivalries, and the crosscurrents of politics as are most adult institutions. In some respects it seems to perpetuate older divisions between students and faculty. But on the whole its record is good, and it illustrates a student concern with international matters which is widespread on American campuses.

The institute operating within the framework of student government at Stanford is only one approach to the organization by students of campus activities which are concerned with international relations. At the University of Florida the chief arm of the student association is the Cabinet of the President of the Student Council; in the cabinet is a Secretary of International Relations with responsibility for vitalizing and coordinating campus enterprises in his field. In other institutions a committee

---

[5] Institute of International Relations, *A General Handbook of Information* (Stanford University, 1955), p. 2.

is set up, composed of the heads of clubs interested in world affairs. The method and political machinery vary greatly and need to be adapted to local conditions, but the coordination is widely recognized as a concern of student government.

Certain general observations should be made about student government responsibilities. It is unfortunately true on most campuses, and particularly in the larger universities, that a minority of students are involved in student government operations; the civic lethargy which is such a drain on the vitality of adult democratic societies has its counterpart in college communities. It is a continuing task of student leaders, fully recognized by many of them, to reduce the lethargy and to bring larger numbers of students into the activities of organized campus life. A comparable situation exists within the faculty. Too frequently a minority of energetic students, often motivated by earnest civic conscience, work well with a small coterie of faculty members who cooperate with the dean of students, while large numbers of students and large numbers of faculty hold aloof from organized campus life. Whatever the motives or the justifications of those who hold aloof, the result on the life of the institution is unfortunate.

As will be illustrated later, student government works for the greatest benefit of college life when it is student participation in college government, and when faculty and students work cooperatively in the formulation of policy and in the conduct of campus affairs. This cooperation seems to be increasing steadily on campuses throughout the nation. On the bases of the surveys made since 1950 in connection with the Carnegie Endowment program, of direct observation in the field, and of the available literature it seems true that many student associations contribute effectively to the organization of college life, and that one of the areas in which they are most concerned and most successful is that of informal education about world affairs.

A final suggestion may be made. Too frequently student

leaders and their faculty counselors are preoccupied with the immediate day-by-day affairs of student life. An arm of the student association which is concerned with continuing and sustained analysis of the life of the college is seriously needed in most institutions. Associations frequently develop programs for the training of their own oncoming leaders; many of these institutes or classes or apprenticeship programs in campus leadership are intellectually and politically impressive. They reduce the hazard of incontinuity which arises from the rapid turnover of the student population. To these programs in leadership training—indeed, as a part of these programs—there should be added a form of research bureau, an agency for continuing analysis of the college life. Sociological and political studies of campus activities, clubs, publications, strengths and weaknesses would yield excellent returns. They should be conducted jointly by students and faculty members. Among such studies should be regular surveys, inventories, appraisals, and proposals on campus achievements and potentialities in education about world affairs.

The National Student Association

The form and program of student associations on many campuses have been markedly influenced in recent years by the rise of the United States National Student Association. Organizations of students, known ordinarily as Student Unions, have existed in European countries for many years, and there were sporadic efforts to create such an organization in the United States during the 1920's and 1930's. At the risk of undue generalization one may say that before 1930 a general affiliation of students in the United States failed because it had little to build on except social and recreational interests plus local campus politics. During the distressed 1930's movements in this direction were abortive primarily because of the naïveté of many student leaders and the propagandistic influence of some off-campus agencies. During this period academic Americans were repeatedly embarrassed by the activities of self-appointed representatives of American students at international conferences; it became increasingly important for American students to organize on a national basis if they were to participate in international student affairs.

In 1947 a United States National Student Association was formed which has, on the whole, developed with integrity, seriousness, and strength. By 1955 its membership included the student associations of about four hundred campuses, representing more than half the students registered in the nation's accredited colleges and universities. Its annual summer conference attracted in 1955 some eight hundred participants, and its program gave full evidence of the mood of responsible maturity which has arisen among students. The association exercises great and favorable influence on many campuses, and in particular it has become a force in the international relations of American students.

The preamble to the association's constitution is indicative of the nature of the association. It reads:

We, the students of the United States of America, desiring
    to maintain academic freedom and student rights,
    to stimulate and improve democratic student governments,
    to develop better educational standards, facilities, and teaching methods,
    to improve student cultural, social, and physical welfare,
    to promote international understanding and fellowship,
    to guarantee to all people, because of their inherent dignity as individuals, equal rights and possibilities for primary, secondary, and higher education regardless of sex, race, religion, political belief, or economic circumstance,
    to foster the recognition of the rights and responsibilities of students to the school, the community, humanity, and God,
    and to preserve the interests and integrity of the government and Constitution of the United States of America

do hereby establish this Constitution of the United States National Student Association.[6]

In pursuance of these objectives, the association carries on an extensive program, illustrated in the functions of its officers. Each year it elects, in addition to a student president, five vice-presidents who are responsible respectively for programs dealing with National Affairs, Student Government, Student Affairs, Educational Affairs, and International Affairs. A number of these officers give full time to this work during the year they are in office. The association maintains a well-staffed headquarters in Philadelphia, issues a monthly *Bulletin*[7] and a *Newsletter*, carries on an extensive travel program as has been indicated, participates in conferences and conventions of major associations dealing with higher education, maintains close contact with its member campuses, and expresses student viewpoints on appropriate national issues. It is advised by a national board including such figures as Ralph Bunche, Erwin D. Canham, and Eleanor Roosevelt. Since 1954, under grants from the Ford Foundation, it has carried on extensive field studies in the analysis of student life and of students' participation in campus activities.

Since its establishment the National Student Association has been deeply concerned with international matters.[8] Indeed, a main impetus to its organization was the rising interest of students in international matters coupled with the confused situation respecting American relations to student groups and activities in other countries. In general, association interests in international relations have shown themselves in three ways: (1) the stimulation and coordination of student interests and

[6] As quoted in United States National Student Association, *Student Government Bulletin*, November 1954, p. 29.

[7] See *Student Government Bulletin*, published monthly between September and June, by the United States National Student Association, 1234 Gimbel Building, Ninth and Chestnut Sts., Philadelphia.

[8] See *International Affairs, U.S. National Student Association* (Cambridge, Mass.: International Affairs Commission, The Association, 1955).

activities and projects in this field on individual campuses which are associated with NSA; (2) the expression of student points of view to adult groups at the national level; and (3) conduct of the relations of organized American students with students in other countries, including services to American students traveling abroad. While programs in these areas are determined at the annual conferences of the association, the administration of the work has centered in the office of the Vice-President for International Affairs, located in Cambridge, Massachusetts. In the Cambridge office are administered not only the pertinent aspects of the association's program, but also the research and clearinghouse services financed by foundation grants. With a full-time staff and a far-flung program, the office has become the main channel through which organized American students meet their counterparts abroad and participate in a complex network of international relations among students.

The work of the National Student Association in organizing and facilitating summer travel tours for American students has been described in the preceding chapter. Two other phases of its work, centered in the Cambridge office, should be described here—its operations designed to improve and coordinate campus activities bearing on international relations, and its participation in the international activities of student associations. In both these areas the association serves a valuable stimulating and coordinating function.

Believing that "the informal extracurricular activities of campus life have much to do with shaping student interest and activities in international relations and that student government has a major role to play in stimulating and coordinating these activities," the International Relations Commission of the National Student Association very early assumed responsibilities in this field. It became an agency for the exchange among campuses of information and ideas and evaluations in this field; in 1953, and in revised and expanded form in 1954, it issued a special publication on *How to Run a Campus International Program.*[9] On request of members of the association, the commission secured a special grant of foundation funds in 1954 for the employment of a full-time field agent to work with individual student associations in developing a well-rounded and coordinated program of activities concerned with international relations. A number of pilot projects were launched on various campuses. A special service was instituted by the commission to provide college newspapers with a wide range of articles and stories about student life around the world, about student travel, and about the international activities of student groups.

The work of the field agent on campuses concerns itself with the coordination of local activities, with the facilitating of student travel, and with the integration of foreign students into campus life. Paralleling these interests, the commission recommends that individual student associations should establish: (1) a Campus International Coordinating Committee composed of representatives of all organizations concerned with world affairs, (2) a Campus Travel Coordinating Committee, and (3) a Campus Foreign Student Orientation Committee, and that these three be interrelated under "one person, comparable to the 'Secretary of State' for the campus."

The commission recognizes fully the importance of securing able people to work on a campus international relations program and has made arrangements both to provide training for qualified students and to reward successful students by prestige and advancement. The booklet by Lunn sagaciously suggests:

A final word should be said about personnel. To attract qualified individuals to carry out the international relations program, the student government and participating groups must make the positions connected with the program desirable in terms of prestige and advancement. Positions in the program cannot be "dead-end" jobs if top-notch people are to be recruited. Instead, efficient service in this area should be rewarded with further opportunities in other parts of

[9] Harry H. Lunn, Jr., *How to Run a Campus International Program* (Cambridge, Mass.: International Affairs Commission, The Association, 1954).

student government and campus organizations. The international program may serve, as well, as initial training for students interested in participating in work with the USNSA International Commission. Fifteen students from all parts of the U.S. have been given all-expense scholarships to the International Student Seminar at Harvard for the 1954 summer program, and the same opportunity will be open year after year to qualified students. A campus program can be excellent training ground for the Seminar, and this should be pointed out to students who are interested in the program.

From the Seminar, in turn, the USNSA obtains representatives for serving at international meetings. USNSA national officers and staff members have many times received training through the Seminar.[10]

The seminar is a six-week session conducted at the commission headquarters each summer under the management of the commission staff and with the cooperation of specialists in a number of related fields. It is an outstanding example of the thoughtful training of promising student leaders.

The operations of the National Student Association at the international level are central to the association's purpose. Among student groups as among most other groups with international contacts, there have been, during the last decade, strong reflections of the international conflict of ideologies and power. The United States National Student Association has from its beginning rejected affiliation with Communist-dominated student groups and has been instrumental in establishing the International Student Conference (ISC) and its agency, the Coordinating Secretariat of National Unions of Students (COSEC). This association holds an annual conference, publishes a monthly bulletin during the academic year, and conducts field studies and investigations into the welfare of students throughout the world.

At the 1955 meeting of the International Student Conference, held in Birmingham, England, students from more than fifty countries were in attendance. They encountered difficulties in seating delegates, in determining an agenda, in dealing with

[10] *Ibid.*, p. 11.

committee reports, and in formulating policies and program directives—all in the manner of adults at any international conference. Commissions on (1) the "basis of cooperation" among different national unions, (2) travel and student exchange, (3) press and information, (4) the work of international delegations, (5) seminars and cultural activities, (6) faculty and specialist activities, (7) social and educational affairs, and (8) implementation of cooperation filled ten days with intensive work for the delegates. All the merits which attach to model United Nations assemblies are present in realistic form in such annual conferences as that held in Birmingham, affording several hundred student leaders valuable apprentice experience in the conduct of cultural, and sometimes political, affairs at an international level.

The National Student Association has become an organization of permanent influence in American academic life. Its influence is particularly effective in the out-of-class activities by which students acquire ideas and attitudes and experience in international affairs. It is in some respects a proving ground for adult leaders of civic affairs both on the national and the international scene. It has taken student leadership in organizing the life of American colleges and universities and has established relations, intelligently conducted, with student groups throughout the free world.

Joint Student-Faculty Action

Faculty as well as students during recent decades have become increasingly interested in organizing and improving college life. Administrative action and faculty counsel have been helpful in establishing the systems of student government on virtually every campus on which they exist. Many institutions have established faculty committees on student life. As was pointed out in chapter 1, the development of the offices and functions of deans of students has led toward the integration of contemporary college life. While in some cases faculty action designed to improve college life has been unilateral in character, so to speak, much of the action has been undertaken cooperatively with student leaders. Sometimes the cooperation has seemed to students to be adept coercion, but there are marked trends toward fully cooperative action in which both students and faculties accept responsibilities and also limitations on their authority. A number of illustrations of this cooperative approach may be cited.

Developments at Drake University in Iowa illustrate a general trend concerning faculty-student efforts at organizing college life. Student government began at Drake in 1881; by 1904 a "Model Senate" composed of class officers was active; by 1921 it was known as the Student Advisory Board, and in 1942 it became the Student-Faculty Council, "a governing body with wide responsibilities and influence on the campus, composed of eight students and seven faculty members." [11] The council holds weekly sessions and is responsible through a series of committees for the coordination and in some cases the actual operation of the out-of-class activities of college life. Its committees manage the campus chest, arrange university convocations, coordinate social affairs, and are responsible for a number of special events. It recommends policies on such matters as library services and athletic facilities. It has a special group working on student-faculty relations:

> The Student-Faculty Council, considered a decade ago to be somewhat of an "experiment," has now gone far beyond that stage and become a meaningful and contributing part of the university's program. Important as are its many co-curricular contributions to campus life and the opportunity for working in campus government, its greatest significance lies in its provision of a shared student and faculty experience. Striving side-by-side, honestly seeking and learn-

[11] Robert B. Kamm, "A Student-Faculty Approach to Campus Government," *School and Society,* June 12, 1954, p. 186.

ing together, participating student and faculty members have been able to achieve new high levels of understanding and appreciation.[12]

Antioch College in Ohio has a relatively unique organization of college government rooted in the characteristics of the institution's program. Students are admitted to a share in management of all aspects of the organized community life of the college. An Administrative Council, with responsibilities extending to the employment and promotion of faculty, is composed of six faculty members and three students, all elected by all the members of the college community. A comparable Community Council is composed of six students and three faculty members, similarly elected. Administrative officers of Antioch sit as ex offico members of the councils, which are the central authorities of the college.

The Community Council is equivalent to the student government system of most institutions, plus faculty participation in the system. The council, to a degree, regulates and coordinates the life of the college. It employs a full-time community manager, whose relations to the council are those of a city manager to his policy-making board. The manager is an advanced student, who takes over the job during his work period under the Antioch plan. By that plan a student takes classes for three months and then is employed in a field related to his career objective for three months. The community manager is a qualified student, probably majoring in political science, for whom the paid manager's post satisfies his work requirement. Under his administrative guidance a series of committees, each made up of students and faculty, deal with the business services, community services, social action, cultural activities, social program, and general administration of the college as a community. Under the council:

Community government begins, roughly, where the classroom leaves off. It is responsible for the assimilation of newcomers into

[12] *Ibid.*, p. 188.

the Antioch community, and for educating the community concerning the principles on which their group life is based. Through its power over the budget it coordinates campus activities and runs many of them directly. It encourages the habit of community participation. It is responsible, along with the deans of the College, for the social counseling. It does not do these things . . . under the negative premise that the students "take over" various functions in order to avoid administrative control. It works from a positive basis—that of a total student-faculty group trying to explore its common environment and meet its common needs. . . .

The relationship of Community government to the legal organization of the college is informal. Technically, because Antioch operates under a corporate charter from the State of Ohio, Community government functions by delegation of authority from the Administrative Council. Ideologically the source of authority of Community government lies in the will of the citizens of the community—students, faculty, and staff. Practically the Administrative Council has always respected Community government, particularly since issues are never permitted to grow to the point where they create cleavages. This lack of formal status has worked to the advantage of Community government, because it has not been frozen at any stage of its development, but instead has been free to grow as fast as it could demonstrate responsibility.[13]

Student-faculty cooperation at Antioch, which is a spirit and process even more than a political structure, is the source of the strength of the system. However, the very vitality of the college government, fostered by the individualism which is traditional for Antioch students, seems to enhance its concern with local matters. It has not developed as extensive interests in international relations as exist on many other campuses.

An outstanding example of coordinated and cooperative management of college life in a larger institution is found at the University of Minnesota. There the University Senate in 1946 formulated a statement on *Basic University Policy Concerning Student Organizations and Their Activities* which reads, in part:

The University Senate, responsible for formulating educational policies, considers student activities and programs an integral part

---

[13] Algo D. Henderson and Dorothy Hall, *Antioch College: Its Design for Liberal Education* (New York: Harper & Bros., 1946), pp. 161–63.

of the University's total educational program. In order to contribute significantly to students' educational progress, to their recreational needs and to their personal development, student activities should give to participants experiences which yield: stimulation of interest in current social, political, economic, cultural or religious issues and problems; experience in living and working in group projects with individuals of different races, creeds and cultural backgrounds; intellectual development in fields related to classroom experiences; development of professional ideals and standards through activities of a professional type; practice in recognizing and exercising the responsibilities of citizenship; development of personal and professional friendships and associations; development of capacities for leadership in group enterprises; and recreational experiences within the cultural environment of the University.[14]

Noting that both students and faculty have privileges and responsibilities in the life of the college community, and listing types of activities which are appropriate for campus promotion, the Senate statement concludes:

The University has established advisory and supervisory relationships with student groups with regard to the nature of activities, problems of financial management and effective utilization of opportunities to achieve educational, recreational and self-development purposes. Close cooperative working relations should be maintained by student organizations and their members with faculty advisers and with the staff of the Student Activities Bureau which serves as the normal channel for relationships between student organizations and the University administration. The Senate Committee on Student Affairs has general jurisdiction over all matters of policy, regulations, rules and programs relating to student activities. The students at all times have free access to this committee for review and discussion of such matters. The responsibility for administering such policies, rules and regulations and for general supervision over student activities has been assigned by the administration of the University to the Student Activities Bureau in the office of the Dean of Students.[15]

The constructive, positive development of student activities as an educative force which was envisaged in this policy statement in 1946 has evolved since then into a noteworthy university

---

[14] Statement approved by the University Senate of the University of Minnesota, October 31, 1946.
[15] *Ibid.*

enterprise. Student participation in the continuing formulation and application of policies has steadily increased. The Office of the Dean of Students has taken on pertinent functions, including that of continual research and analysis of student life.

The Office of the Dean of Students includes the Bureau of Student Loans and Scholarships, the Bureau of Veterans Affairs, the Coordinator of Students' Religious Activities, the Foreign Student Services, a Speech and Hearing Clinic operated as a part of the university's Personnel Service, the Student Activities Bureau, a Student Counseling Bureau, and a Student Housing Bureau. The *Students' Handbook* for 1954 indicates that the Student Activities Bureau "is to aid and advise students in planning their activities, handling group funds and training officers." It is an advisory center for individual students who seek a part in student activities. With a staff composed partly of young graduates who have emerged as student leaders at the University of Minnesota and partly of people recruited from other campuses, the bureau keeps in touch with all student organizations, cooperates in their enterprises, carries on sociological analysis of them and their role in the university, and makes suggestions to the organizations for improving their operations. The bureau has contributed substantially both to the morale of the campus and to the educative level of student activities.

The structure and operation of the dean's office and specifically of the Student Activities Bureau at the University of Minnesota are, of course, unique to that institution. The important point is not the specific machinery for accomplishing an objective but the fact that the objective has so clearly become a part of institutional policy and philosophy. In many other colleges and universities the same objectives are sought by administrative arrangements appropriate to the institution's structure and resources and tradition.

Within the complex university life of the large group of students and faculty at Minnesota there is no single center for the promotion and coordination of activities concerned with world affairs. But in the offices of the Bureau of Student Affairs and in programs reaching into clubs, fraternities and sororities, the religious groups, the development of campus events, the organization of philanthropies, and the management of the university union, a wide range of activities dealing with international affairs are brought within an organized framework. The life of the university, as has been indicated in the account of the student travel program known as SPAN, is well weighted with international interests.

Conclusion

Student activities which are carried on for activity's sake, no matter how strenuous and exciting they may be, are hardly the materials for constructing a justifiable college life. Even the activities and enterprises which are worthy of higher education have only a haphazard influence so long as they are left to chance or are fragmented and proliferated. Organization of campus activities simply for the sake of system and orderliness is also only of trifling value. It is the thesis of this volume, however, that many of the non-class activities in college life are intellectually and aesthetically legitimate as well as challenging, and that, by taking thought, their importance may be enhanced to the benefit of higher education. Indeed, the traditional functions of the college and university cannot be adequately served in our kind of society except as worthy activities are cultivated on the campus.

The cultivation of activities which elevate the life of the campus is fully as much the responsibility of a faculty which is sensitive to the teaching function as it is the responsibility of students. Cultivation of college life as a deeply educative experience involves a sense of the college as a community, a conviction that there is no rigid dividing line between class and out-of-class experience, an assumption that as wisdom is knowledge in action, so college learning is motivated and vitalized by doing. It is here assumed that the total way of college life educates the members of the college and that no full program of collegiate education can ignore the informal any more than it can ignore the formal influences of the campus. In no sense does this thesis pit extraclass against class activities; it but emphasizes that each is enriched by a strong relation between the two. Only as this relationship is developed can there be consistency among the formative influences of higher education. Only as both activities and instruction are directed toward a common goal of education can the college or university exercise its major influence on students.

For one who is concerned with college level education about world affairs, informal campus activities are of special importance. Not only may they bulwark and enrich classroom instruction about national cultures and international relations for those students who enroll for such instruction, but they may also reach large numbers of students who are not now touched at all by specific courses in international relations. If one assumes that no student should graduate from college or university whose mind and spirit have not been quickened and enlightened in their grasp of international relations, it becomes essential to develop the extracurriculum and the cocurriculum as well as the curriculum to that end.

The college or university as a place, a set of buildings, and a physical environment, conditions the informal education of its members, including their education about world affairs. If a college is a place of beauty, it strikes aesthetic chords within those who call it alma mater; some of those chords may be struck by items of beauty and sentiment on the campus which are symbolic of ties with other cultures. But beyond this valid emotional base, the physical facilities for learning which exist on the campus determine and shape the pattern of feasible activities by which students learn. The library, the assembly hall, the chapel, the clubroom, the college union, the international house or center may be made instruments of conscious education exactly as a classroom can. Not just by chance, but by high-visioned programing may these facilities of learning be made to contribute to college education, including college education about world affairs.

In developing a college program of education about world affairs, it should be recognized that the modern institution has not only physical but also human resources which condition the program. The American campus through the members of the college is intimately related to far-flung cultures and to the management of foreign policies and international relations; living in the college group may itself be an education in world affairs if the potentialities of the groups of foreign students, of widely traveled faculty members, and of faculty members who have participated in the foreign relations of the national government or the work of international organizations are adequately used.

It continues to be true that college life is a mixture of valuable and valueless enterprises, but it is also true that the better of these activities contribute substantially to lifting the level of college life. The number of student clubs which are extensions and supplements of the formal curriculum is considerable, and the zest which many students accord to these enterprises is encouraging. A detailed description of the lectures, forums, exhibits, concerts, film showings, discussions, debates, and conversations in the life of any college for a day or week would evidence the merit of much of this activity and the possibilities of its further improvement. The same thing would be revealed by analysis of the travel habits of students on any campus for the cycle of one or four years. In these activities are the elements for producing a finer college life and a more effective program of education about world affairs than most institutions have yet realized. Through all these informal activities, as well as through classes and seminars, the student may learn much about national cultures and cultural contacts, about foreign policies and current affairs, and about the processes of international relations. In the context of all these activities the college makes its contribution to the ideas and attitudes, orientations and values by which students see the world about them.

But if all these activities run riot on a campus, they are likely to be reflected in scatterbrained students moving energetically in all directions. Only as the manifold activities and influences of the campus may be interrelated to provide unity, coordinated to avoid conflict and duplication, and focused on objectives of international understanding which are worthy of educated men and women, can the life of the institution reach its highest level. As has been seen in earlier pages of this chapter, groups of students and of faculties and of administrators are now moving in the direction of ordering and focusing the activities of college life. There is reason for hope in the developments of current years that the college and university of the future will reintegrate the life of the institution and cultivate its potentialities, formal and informal, in such fashion as to give wisdom greater prestige in its mores and traditions. In that process the education of American students about world affairs may be attained in a degree reasonably related to the demands for international understanding now placed upon them.

Index

Date Due

DEC 1 9 '80			
OCT 2 '62			
𝒢𝓑	PRINTED	IN U. S. A.	

Studies in
Universities and
World Affairs